IN SEARCH OF THE

Jesus People

IN SEARCH OF THE

Jesus People

DAVID GERVAIS

ARPress
ILLUMINATING IDEAS.
EMPOWERING VOICES

ARPress
45 Dan Road Suite 5
Canton MA 02021
Hotline: 1(888) 821-0229
Fax: 1(508) 545-7580

Ordering Information:
Quantity sales. Special discounts are available on quantity purchases by corporations, associations, and others. For details, contact the publisher at the address above.

Printed in the United States of America.

ISBN-13:	Softcover	979-8-89330-294-3
	eBook	979-8-89330-293-6

Library of Congress Control Number: 2024901463

TABLE OF CONTENTS

FOREWORD
RONN HAGUE

Pearl River Community College Digital Media Coordinator/Museum Director, Author, Composer, Speaker, and Filmmaker

Having known some of the characters in this wonderful book, I was excited to read it. I was not disappointed. The author captures the "feeling" of the time, because right after Hurricane Camille devastated the Mississippi Gulf Coast the whole area experienced a tremendous move of the Holy Spirit during which many thousands of young people were miraculously saved and transformed.

That era was marked by witnessing on the beach, Jesus Rock Festivals in the parks, and a sudden surge in home Bible study and prayer groups. David Gervais recaptures this era and the spiritual atmosphere beautifully. This book allowed me to revisit a wonderful and blessed part of my life.

For the reader who has never experienced a move of the Holy Spirit, this book outlines the amazing things that transpire. The author does a great job of creating the sense of wonder that prevailed during this time. David's conversion experience and the resulting life transformation attest to the power of a risen Lord.

I also appreciate his honesty about the personal trauma he was subjected to, which, I believe, may help others who experienced similar events at the hand of so-called religious people—people who Jesus warned us about in Matthew 7:15, ". . . false prophets, which come to you in sheep's clothing, but inwardly they are ravening wolves." (KJV)

The Lord used all of these events, good and bad, to produce in David a fine Christian minister, musician, and writer who is using all the wonderful gifts he has been given to the glory of God.

FROM THE AUTHOR

This book is dedicated to people who want to know God at a deeper level but may have been misled by religious radicalism or authoritarian leaders. Perhaps you or someone you love knows people who have dealt with cults. Possibly even you have been a victim of their misaligned and untruthful ways.

A person familiar with cults, who views them objectively from within and without, will understand their destructive tendencies over time. To those whose lives have been impacted or even trapped by religious groups gone astray, and have been fortunate and blessed enough to escape their clutches, I want to say, you are not alone in what you have experienced, and you are to be congratulated for the courage you have shown.

These groups can seem refreshing and alive to those who are not grounded in a faith system that works, or who have been discouraged and disappointed frequently within unfulfilling religious dogma or ritualistic formula. Young people may be particularly vulnerable, and many become ensnared. Remember, too, that most of the time no one considers themselves to actually be part of a cult. The group's teachings will usually have just enough truth to deceive willing or naïve people.

While this is my story, it may be your story, too, or the story of someone you care deeply about. Assurance in times of dealing with cults comes from truth, and the Lord has a way of leading His children toward that truth. "Let not your heart be troubled." There is hope. There is faith. There is a future for you, though your vision may have become clouded with despair and confusion, as mine was when I first made that unthinkable choice to leave the cult that had captured me.

Sometimes you just have to take a stand and do the courageous thing. Sometimes you just have to boldly face the truth which has been right in front of you. After your decision to separate from them, you'll slowly realize that you've been part of closed and distanced hierarchies, false teaching, and isolated existence. If you'll keep an open heart, you'll realize that God has been with you the whole time and your eyes will gradually open to brighter days ahead.

If this book helps you better understand cults and become more adept at dealing with them for yourself or for those you love, read on. You might just love to sit down and read an interesting story. Either way, this informative sequence of events may just be the eye-opening drama and revelation you've been waiting for.

ACKNOWLEDGEMENTS

Special thanks to God for giving the necessary inspiration to put this story into words. Thanks, also, to my parents for having raised me in the way of the Lord, teaching by example the importance of weekly church attendance.

My sister, Cathy, put in many hours going over each chapter and bringing the words to vibrant life. Her contribution was comparable to converting a black and white movie to living color.

I pray that prospective readers will be both entertained and informed by the dramatic turn of events which took place around 39 years ago. Written in a fictional format, this book is based on true occurrences, although most names have been changed or altered.

The dangers of cult activity, however, are still all too real in the world today. As you turn the pages and immerse yourself in the story, be entertained and inspired, but allow God to speak gently to your heart to steer you away from any teaching which is not spiritually healthy for the human soul. The Gospel of our Lord Jesus Christ is more than sufficient, and is still providing grace to all who call upon God.

LEAVING A CULT
A BOY'S JOURNEY TO LIFE IN CHRIST PROLOGUE

As I hurriedly walked toward the exit door of our small, hometown grocery store, the A & P in Long Beach, Mississippi, holding my clip on tie in one hand, I snatched my tightly tucked in shirt out of my pants with my free hand. "See ya tomorrow Kenny!" I called out to one of my co-workers who had taken over the task of bagging groceries.

"Later man!" Kenny smiled back at me as he tucked the canned goods into the brown paper sacks with the large, red letters that proudly proclaimed: "The A & P thanks you and come again!"

Ah, it was a good feeling to be getting off of work early. I had been hired as a bag boy three years earlier, shortly after turning sixteen. "Where are you off to in such an all-fired-rush?" asked Kenny.

"I'm going to some kind of concert at the high school. Cathy told me about it" I replied. Cathy was my younger sister who was a sophomore at the local high school. Paul, a friend of ours, had organized the event to take place during the high school's activity period. They were both all excited over the big concert!

The breeze from the beach was warm and brisk today. The unmistakable sea scent was as familiar to me as the large, white gulls that flew above, dipping down into the parking lot for a dropped French fry or other small tidbit left behind by the shoppers, squawking happily on this beautiful day. "Ok birds; fly away from my new car!" I said quietly to myself, hoping I didn't have a mess to clean up on my spic and span 1974 chocolate brown Maverick Grabber. I beamed with pride at my first new car as I put the keys into the ignition and started the engine. The radio was blaring one of my favorite songs. Barely glancing at the frothy white caps on the ocean across the road, I whipped out of the parking lot, tapping my hand to the song's beat on the steering wheel and setting out toward the high school.

When I arrived, the bleachers in the gym were already rapidly filling up with excited school kids who were glad to have a break from regular classes. The noises of their voices echoed off the concrete block walls. I quickly located my sister and her friends and went over to sit next to them for the concert.

"Glad you could get off work, Dave! The concert will be starting soon now." She said smiling and waving to one of her friends and tossing her long brown hair over her shoulders. Cathy was an outgoing, pretty girl who had made friends easily since she was very young. The boys noticed her at an early age, and as she developed into a teenager, she had many admirers. She was quite a talented singer. She and I had long enjoyed making music for the Lord together, me on the piano and she singing. I had learned the piano early, picking it up naturally and easily.

Looking up at the stage, I watched as several teenaged boys walked in wearing stylish black leisure suits and wide collared colorful jersey shirts; each going to a different instrument as they prepared to play their first song. A young looking lady made her way to the microphone and said, "Praise the Lord! It's so good to be here in Long Beach, Mississippi!" Then the crisp "Click, click, click" of the drumsticks sounded giving the beat to the band members. The music began to roar throughout the gymnasium as an upbeat version of a popular hymn was performed, in a way that I'd never before heard. The song came to a close and the woman again said, "Praise the Lord!" as the crowd of stunned teenagers clapped thunderously. "My name is Judy and we're the Rejoice singers." She said smiling and proceeded to introduce the rest of the group.

She had two sons and two nephews in the band, who played instruments and sang, and two other members who were unrelated. Her oldest nephew, Steve, then announced their next song as he began to play his guitar. He had a strong, mellow voice and sang solo on the verses and then Steve's younger brother, David joined in on the chorus. Again, the music reverberated through the entire gym, setting the students on the edges of their seats. The thirty-minute concert flew by when in closing, an especially uplifting song, with a haunting melody began to play. The beautiful voices of this talented trio blended together singing the heart-felt words: "He can fill an ocean; He can hold your hand when you're alone." The song swelled and built, like the sea as the presence and peace of God filled my heart. For a few brief moments, I felt as though I was the only person in that entire gymnasium. My heart filled with joy and love for the Lord. At that moment, I knew that he would be ever present in the lives of His children, even in their darkest hour!

His hand of guidance and protection doesn't leave simply because we as humans are unable to feel it at any given moment. God had certainly been with me through some mighty dark days in the past couple of years of my life!

The present month and year was May 1975, but my mind wandered back to an earlier date. A full year had already passed since my family and I had walked away from a place that people around here called, "The Farm". My mind had been capable of taking me to places far away from the reality of this world, since I was a small boy. But that was before . . . before the unspeakable had happened, which had ripped from me the precious gift of even a simple daydream. I had been trapped in a nightmare, unable to escape the torment of the pain inflicted on my weary mind.

It was the fall of 1972. I was still a senior in high school, naive and lonely; hungering for all that had been missing in my life. I began to search for more in my soul, more than just religion and dogma. I wanted to find peace, love, the light of God and a way to walk in that light. It was this search that eventually led me to the "the House of Praise", a place which was no more than a large old farmhouse built by a lovely, tranquil lake in a wooded area, off the beaten path. To the innocent onlooker, it was a place out of a Norman Rockwell painting, complete with a tire swing in the back yard hanging from an old, moss-strewn oak tree.

CHAPTER 1

THE SEARCH

But seek ye first the kingdom of God
And His righteousness . . . Matthew 6:33

A s I made my way down the familiar halls of Long Beach High, I felt a crisp, cool breeze blow down the hall. It was 1972; the sky was a brilliant robin's egg blue. It was the kind of day that made one feel good to be alive! The entire student body crammed the busy hallways heading toward the gym for our Friday afternoon pep rally. The slamming of the gray school lockers mixed with the voices and laughter as a pretty girl wearing a bright red maxi dress swished past me, her long brown hair tied into a low ponytail at the base of her neck. "Hey Dave" a soft voice said as the girl smiled at me in passing. "Hey Becky" I answered quietly, my voice being quickly muffled by the peals of laughter and foot stomping inside the gym. The kids couldn't wait for the rally to begin, the fall air making spirits even higher than usual.

The teenage boys had long hair swooping down over their foreheads and blue jeans, some with patches sewn on the back pockets; the American flag was very popular, as was the peace sign and the smiley face. The once crisp button down oxford cloth shirts now were wrinkled from slouching in desks all day. A tall boy with curly blond hair and ruddy complexion walked toward me, the button on his shirt catching my attention read: I'm a Jesus People! A flash of last week's evening newscast went through my mind. Our local news station had done a clip featuring the "Jesus People" out in California. The fresh scrubbed boy with the button on his shirt bore no resemblance to the dancing hippies on the television, all proclaiming in a dazed state to be "Jesus People". They more resembled something out of a rock concert and were questionable at best.

The blond haired boy and his clean cut friends walked into the loud gymnasium in front of me and we all settled on the same row of bleachers that had been pulled out from the walls to accommodate the rowdy students. Not being much of a sports fan, I still enjoyed cheering for the home team of the Long Beach Bearcats, but in truth, the band and cheerleaders perked my interest far more than the long, dull football game. As the cheerleaders came running out onto the wooden gym floor, I pushed my hair out of my eyes to get a better view.

The clapping and cheering was contagious as I began to chant the class yell: *"We're the best as you can see! Senior class of '73!"* The roaring, clapping and stomping on the bleachers made a thunderous noise, almost drowning out the entire brass section of the band. The long day of hum drum school lessons faded away along with the fact that in a bit more than an hour, I would be back at the good ole local grocery store; bagging for the customers, trying to remember not to crush the loaves of bread under the canned peas.

The walk home after the excitement of the pep rally was quiet and peaceful. We lived only a half mile away and I usually opted to either walk or ride my bike to and from school. It was actually quicker than the school bus driven by our four fingered shop teacher. He shifted that old clunky school bus so slow, it felt like I could get out and crawl faster. It was rumored he'd not been the same since that nasty accident with the table saw and one of the Butner boys.

I hummed a tune as I walked through the thick, dried brush in the wooded glen on the way to my house. This year was going to be the best year ever in school for me. I could just feel it! It was the first year I was not going to be stuck in some sweaty Physical Education class, praying that I would not be noticed by the coach when I skulked away to avoid the awkward humiliation of being the very last kid "chosen" for a team sport. Since I was a small boy, I'd endured mortification every time I struggled to play any sort of game that involved a ball. My interests had always been in music, but since my natural voice wouldn't allow me to sing in the school chorus, and my parents couldn't afford the expensive band instruments which were required to participate in the band class, I'd been stuck in P.E. with the sweaty jocks who looked at me with disdain as I fumbled hopelessly with each attempt at any given game.

My love for music was never stronger than when I was playing the piano. Even though I'd only had lessons in the fifth and sixth grade, I'd never forgotten the feeling I had as my fingers touched the smooth ivory keys, with a melody filling the room that came from each tap, tap, tap of my fingers. I'd excelled in typing in school, even winning the award for the fastest and best typist in the entire junior class. It came easily to me, as I imagined the keys on the old typewriter were the creamy white and jet-black keys of the magical piano. Music swirled in my head at nearly every waking moment, sometimes causing my mind to drift from school lessons as I imagined myself either playing the piano, drums, guitar, or any given instrument that was prominent in the song which flowed through my mind like the breeze on this autumn day.

Ah, but this year, *this* year, I was going to take Art! It was the first time this class had been offered and I was among the enthusiastic art loving kids to sign up for it. Just the thought of it made me smile all through the walk home which flew by in what seemed to be seconds.

The Autumn quickly turned to winter when I finally had saved up enough money from bagging groceries at the grocery store to purchase my first car; a 1966 Comet! It was tan and of course worn around the edges, but to me, it was my magic carpet to a whole new world! I could hop in and go places I'd never before been free to visit! On my bicycle I'd been able to peddle as far as the big town of Gulfport to visit the stores that our tiny Long Beach never had. I even had become brave enough to go down the old beach highway, leaving my bike in the dock for cars and walking the sugar white beaches, the ocean lapping at my toes while the sea gulls soared and dipped as the shrimp boats floated by. But a car, well, that was something else all together!

School was proving to be much more tolerable this year with the addition of the art class. I'd met some new friends and enjoyed the many projects of creating something from little of nothing. It helped to satisfy the urge I had to make a creation that fed the soul, rather than just filling the mind with facts and figures.

One day, after finishing our projects, our teacher, Mrs. Russo, allowed us to fill the remaining class time quietly with reading or homework. Julie, a soft spoken and shy dark haired girl that sat next to me was reading a book that caught my eye. It had an erupting volcano in brilliant reds and oranges with big bold letters proclaiming an end time apocalypse.

"Hey Julie, what's that book you're reading, a science fiction?" I whispered in her direction hoping she would hear.

"Are you kidding me? No way!" Julie said furrowing her eyebrows as she began to describe the book with a hushed excitement in her voice. "This is *the* book that's so popular right now that tells about the end times, you know, when the Lord comes back and takes all his children to be with him, but all the people who have not repented are stuck here." She bent over a bit closer, her brown eyes as large as saucers. "It's the author's interpretation, of course, but oh my gosh, it will scare the be-jeeber's right on out of you! If you aren't saved when you start reading this book, I'll bet you by golly will be when you get finished with it! Wow!"

"Ok, back in the peanut gallery, that's enough. Either get quiet or you can come up front and scrub out all the paint brushes." Mrs. Russo ordered.

"Oops!" Julie said, a bit of spit flying out of her new braces. I noticed that she too was wearing one of those "Jesus People" buttons. What was it with all these Jesus buttons anyway, and now this new book? Was this some sort of fad or was there really something to all of it? I decided then and there I'd take that "new" car of mine over to the bookstore in Gulfport the next chance I got and pick up one of those books for myself. I'd get to the bottom of this!

The following weekend after I had come home from work, my mother had arrived just before me. Mama was a petite woman; all of five foot tall and 100 pounds. Long ago she'd been nicknamed "Little-Bit" by her co-workers at the old .5 & .10 store where she had worked in downtown Gulfport. The old store still did a thriving business today and had changed very little from those days in the 1940's when all the merchandise was stacked neatly in dark mahogany bins with glass dividing shelves. The floors were the original black and white small tiles in the art deco style. The only difference now was that in addition to the huge ceiling fans that hung low from the high ceilings, the marvel of modern air conditioning had been added. It was now much more comfortable to sit and dine at the white marble countered lunch bar.

Mama now worked part time at the local dime store which was right next to the grocery store which now employed me. Both businesses faced the mighty Gulf of Mexico on Highway 90.

As she raised her hand to feel her new hair-do, her face grimaced at the touch. "What on earth ever possessed me to get this ridiculous perm and hair dye, I will never know!"

Her short, dark hair looked cute to me, curled about her face. Her Indian heritage showed in the strong facial features. Her normally short hair was not nearly as flattering as the soft curls, but her mind was just as strong as her features and she would surely be cutting off the locks the first chance she got.

"Davey boy, your old Mama is bone tired tonight. How about run to the hamburger stand and get us all a hamburger, now would ya?" She asked with an apologetic tone to her voice. "I just can't stand over that stove and cook tonight. I'll make it up to everyone tomorrow night." She added.

"Sure Mama. I don't mind." I said, my mind racing to the fact that the bookstore in Gulfport wasn't far from our favorite burger joint. I could zip into the bookstore, grab the book and have it to read tonight!

Mama slowly waddled side to side as she did when her legs and feet ached, stopping in front of the brown cookie jar kept on the simple wooden hutch in the small dining area of the kitchen. "Here . . . here's twenty dollars. Now you come straight on back now, ya here?" She said handing me the crisp bill.

"Yes Ma'am." I answered already half way onto the porch, the screen door slapping behind me.

"And don't forget to feed the dog!" Mama added.

I quickly grabbed the nearly empty sack of dog food from the utility building and emptied a small amount into the battered red plastic dog dish. "Gi Gi girl, come here, supper time!" The little black and tan dachshund ran to me as quickly as her tiny legs could move. "Sit; lay down; roll over" came the automatic commands that she knew must be performed before the bowl would hit the ground. She did all three so fast; they all sort of rolled into one command. "Good girl" I said patting her head.

The drive to Gulfport went quickly with the Mighty 690 blaring out some of my favorite tunes as the wind from the beach blew its fresh, salty air into my lungs. My mind wandered back to the halls of high school and conversations I'd overheard where kids used unfamiliar terms such as "the rapture" and "the great tribulation" or "fulfillment of Bible prophecy" as though they had heard them all their lives. What in the world had I been missing? I couldn't pretend to know about these things, yet I refuse to embarrass myself by letting on as though I don't! I *will* learn just exactly what these terms mean and also, just where I fit in with all of this? Haven't I been following God all my life? I thought I had. But what if I haven't? Now there's a new concept. Since the age of seven, I had planned to join the ministry as soon as I became an adult. Still, I'm determined to seek the truth for myself!

"I can't believe those burgers went up to thirty five cents! Of all the gall!" Mama was outraged when I gave her the change from her twenty. Fast food burgers and fries were among the few places our family ever went out to eat at and that was only on occasion. The menu choices were quite limited with either small or jumbo sized hamburgers or hotdogs.

"Well we may just need to stop eating there!" My money conscience father chimed in.

Now we rarely ever 'ate there' to begin with, but any price increases just added to the argument that we should never again darken the doors of that establishment; thereby saving Daddy the thirty-five cents. "It's the nickels and dimes that add up." He used to say.

The theme song of my favorite television program changed the subject as I made my way to the living room to view the popular sitcom.

"Ok Dave, watch your TV Shows, but after that I'm looking forward to that lawyer show cause it's playin' tonight, too. My mother's voice echoed from the kitchen while she cleaned things up, along with the help of my sister Cathy. I had already taken out the garbage, done my homework and a few other household chores which were evenly divided amongst the children.

Daddy lounged on the sofa and was snoring rhythmically within minutes. For a one hundred and thirty pound man, he could snore like a grizzly bear!

Mama perched in her recliner in the corner of the living room while Cathy curled up on the floor beside the couch. There was the sofa, reserved for Daddy; one chair by the living room exit which was usually mine, and a recliner which belonged exclusively to Mama. Our family dog stayed on a rug at the edge of the room, for she had been trained to go no farther.

My mind couldn't concentrate on the old black and white drama that so enthralled both my mother and little sister. I quietly slipped out of the living room and went to the privacy of my own room where I could shut the door and read my new book. I popped a new cassette tape into my stereo and soon the crisp notes from the guitar relaxed me as I sunk into my bunk bed with my new book.

The book opened up pointing to prophecies in the Old Testament which foretold of Jesus and His walk upon this earth two thousand years ago. I read with rapt attention as this author opened up scriptures to me in a way that I had never known before. I soon realized that I would need to plan another little escape trip to the bookstore in Gulfport to buy a Bible so that I could follow along with the author's instructions.

Our own family Bible had seen better days and the wording in it was just too complicated for me to understand. Years ago I'd attempted to read the first several chapters of Genesis and soon became lost in the 'begats' as well as the obsolete language. However, this author had suggested starting in the New Testament with the gospel of John.

I glanced at my clock which read 10:00 pm. "Good grief, where did the time go?" Thankfully, I was able to drift off to sleep peacefully.

There would be no need to get up in the night to seek out the medicine chest for a couple of aspirins.

I would invariably wake my light sleeping parents on the nights I had insomnia even though I tried so hard to be as quiet as a mouse. My dad had told me some years back that he often took a couple of aspirin tablets to help him sleep. I was willing to try anything to relieve the sleepless nights of tossing and turning, my body exhausted, but my mind still racing. He'd also suggested clearing my mind of all thoughts and just concentrating on a peaceful scene or some pleasant memory. To my surprise, this worked quite well and I had many opportunities to put this practice to use.

Each night after I'd finished my shift at the store, I actually looked forward to going home and reading my book until it was time for lights out and all quiet in our home. The pages seemed to fly through my fingers, especially when I reached the chapter that detailed an event called the 'rapture' of the Church. There was going to be a time coming to the Earth of great tribulation, he explained. This time of trials would last seven years. He covered this subject in much detail, but the Church, as he called it, would not have to go through this particular tribulation. He said the Lord would come back and "catch away" His people before this period of time.

I could hardly believe my eyes! I found myself reading each word breathlessly, hungering for more! The coming chapters told the many various ways the book of Revelation could be interpreted, and the author explained with simplicity and logic these difficult scriptures in the last book of the Bible. He connected many of these prophecies to current events in a very convincing manner. He, also, put much gravity on the doctrine of being "born again".

"Born again"? What precisely is this born again business all about? Is it something pertaining to how you feel? Or maybe it's something that you do? Could it just be something that a particular religion believes? I want the *truth*! But just who can I talk to about finding this truth? "Ok, we'll just see about this. I'll need to find someone to talk to!" I mumbled to myself as I turned off the light switch and set my book on the small dresser beside my bed. That night the words I'd read whirled through my brain. When was Christ coming back? What about this seven-year tribulation that was to happen after the rapture of the Church? A whole new world of God's prophecies had been opened up to me and my heart was thrilled at the prospect of learning more.

The next day while at work, I couldn't get the burning questions out of my head that had been buzzing around since I began reading this new book. As I bagged groceries for Daphne, I determined to take my break at the same time as she did. She had no idea the great respect that I had for her as a Christian. Daphne was a friendly girl all through high school. She sat opposite me in class and one day I noticed that she was reading her Bible during a quiet moment. She brushed her strawberry blonde hair over her shoulder and off of her neck on that hot summer's day, reading intently and quietly. She was never one to loudly push her faith on anyone and didn't even wear one of the "Jesus People" buttons. She rather just sort of lived it. That humility of spirit had caught my attention.

Daphne's older brother Joe had once surprised me when he'd been asked to lead our class in prayer one night before a bonfire on the beach. He prayed with such sincerity; as though he knew the One to whom he prayed. His simple words touched my heart and impacted me in such a way that I'd tucked this memory away deep inside of my heart, never forgetting it. The lit bonfire against the deep, dark summer night twinkling with stars, the breeze from the ocean and the sound of the waves as they broke on the sands still warm from the sun, and a prayer to our Lord in heaven who made them all, thanking Him for the privilege of enjoying our bounty of blessings. I wanted to know more of this Jesus of Nazareth who walked on waters, and was a fisher of men's souls.

Yes, this was a family of deep faith, the kind of faith that I wanted to learn more about.

"I'm ready for my break, girl, come give me some relief!" Daphne joked with Rita, the young girl that was filling in as a break cashier. The two girls smiled and joked happily as Daphne squeezed by to exit the bagging area. I finished bagging the groceries as quickly as possible and rolled the buggy into the parking lot to load them into the customer's car.

"Thank you Dave, now you tell your Mama that I said hey, now ya hear?" Mrs. Taylor said dropping a quarter into my hand for my tip.

"Yes Ma'am and thank you." I answered. I quickly wheeled the buggy back to the store and bounced it roughly into the outside rack. I made my way casually to the break room where Daphne sat, her feet up on the battered coffee table and drinking a Coke.

"Hey Dave, time for your break too, huh?" Daphne asked smiling at me.

"Yeah, it's about that time." I answered. As I put my dime into the drink machine, I turned toward her. "Hey Daphne, I got something to ask you." I said pulling my bottle of icy cold coke from the machine. Course I think it might have been a grape soda. To us southerners, all soft drinks were generically referred to as coke.

Daphne looked up, noticing the change in my voice. "Yeah?" She asked.

"Well, just how can a person know for sure if they are going to heaven?" I blurted out as though I'd just asked her how the weather was.

Daphne set her coke down and thought for a few seconds before answering "Well Dave, you just have to accept it by faith. If you've asked Jesus into your life, you just have to believe that you're saved." She answered simply.

You mean it's just as simple as that, I thought to myself. I'd expected something a bit more philosophical and complicated than that.

My thoughts were abruptly cut off when a giant wad of wet paper towels flew across the room and smacked Daphne squarely in the face.

"Rooster, I'm gonna get you good, man!" Daphne squealed, half in shock and half in sheer delight.

Daphne loved a good joke as well as the next person and Maurice; aka "Rooster" was the top prankster around the store. His nickname suited him. His flaming red hair looked just like a rooster cone sticking straight up in the air several inches. His freckles that covered his face matched his hair, and he wore a grin as big as the sun. You couldn't help but smile back at him when you saw him coming. Daphne went flying out of the break room in hot pursuit of the prankster.

I chuckled to myself at their antics when suddenly the intercom system for the break room blared loudly "Woods . . . we need package help up front right now! Your break is officially OVER! Now hustle your back side up to the front!"

Gulping down the last drops of my drink I scrambled to get up the isle toward the front of the store. The separate intercom system for the store then interrupted the soft elevator style music with an announcement. "We need package help on the front register, please." The kind voice dripped with politeness. It was hard to believe it was the same assistant manager that just ripped me over the break room intercom. Oh how I just wish that one fine day, he'd put his chubby finger on the wrong button and make his rude announcement over the store speaker. I just wonder how that would go over with the manager, who was also Daphne's father. Well, the thought of that little scenario made me smile as I quickly began to bag the groceries for the annoyed shoppers.

Willie, another red haired classmate of mine who had just started working as a bag boy came in from the parking lot dripping wet with a miserable look on his face. I looked out of the plate glass windows to see that a thunderstorm had quickly rolled in from the Gulf. This always had the magical effect of flushing all the beach goers off of the sandy beach and into the grocery store. The store was cram packed with shoppers. The lady I was now bagging groceries for was a black lady with a three-year-old child. The two seemed to be thoroughly enjoying one another's company.

"Grandma, what cha' lookin' for, huh? The adorable dark eyed girl looked up at her Grandma as she searched the candy rack

"Well I can't find it, dog gone." The black lady said gently with a smile.

"Dog gone" the little girl repeated, her cheeks creased with a dimple on each side.

"Yeah baby, dog gone." The lady said laughing and picking up the little girl, kissing her on the cheek.

I'd bagged the groceries of this kind woman many times before and she always had a nice word to say and a smile for me. I secretly wondered if she were one of those "born-again" Christians. Maybe I would ask her some day.

Meanwhile, my school life took on a new dimension. I actively sought out conversations with teens that were willing to talk about what being a Christian meant to them and how it changed their lives. With all my heart and soul, I wanted to serve and walk with the Lord Jesus Christ. Of course, I still tried to appear cool and casual when I started the conversations. I had not lost sense of the fragile social status of the average teen in high school.

I'd finished the book I'd bought, dog-earing the pages with the most interesting points that I would re-read over and over again, along with the given scriptures. I'd gotten my very first Bible, just a little paperback New Testament which was a newer English translation, allowing me to better understand the wording. It was already showing wear from the studying I was doing each night in the quiet and privacy of my little room.

After watching an evangelist on television one night, I decided to go to my room to be in private with my thoughts. "Good night Mama. See you in the morning." I said getting up from my usual chair.

"Oh, good night Dave. Hope you sleep good." My mother answered with a sleepy yawn. My father snored contentedly on his sofa.

My heart was burning with conviction as I opened my tiny Bible. I couldn't concentrate on the words I read. "Ok, I'm just going to put aside all my fears and uncertainty. I've wavered long enough!" I mumbled to myself. I needed to ask Jesus to give me the assurance of salvation. I knew this with every fiber of my being. My greatest fear had been that if I surrendered all to the Lord, he would compel me to become a priest. Although at the age of seven, I had proclaimed to all my intentions of joining the priesthood, my teen years had seen that desire fade long ago. Even though I loved God and wanted to serve him, I held back this final, most personal part of my life. But now, I was willing to follow wherever he may lead. I'd searched for the truth, and I'd found it.

Closing my Bible I slid to my knees beside my bed, bowing my head in reverence. I tried to word the prayer as close to the ones I'd read in various salvation tracts. The room was still and silent as my heart-felt words pierced the quiet.

"Lord Jesus, I believe you are the Son of God and came to this earth to die for my sins. I ask that you forgive me and come into my heart. I give my life to you Lord. Amen." I looked up through my tears into the same little room that I'd known all my life. But somehow, it was different now. I felt the Lord had heard my prayer and His presence filled my heart and flowed out from me, like a gentle breeze. My new life in Christ had just begun.

In the following days, I noticed subtle changes in my life. The locker-room language I'd picked up during my years of P.E. now left a bad taste in my mouth. The words which had become a part of my normal vocabulary now were disappearing as a sense of sadness and guilt would well up from within me every time questionable language would escape. Something told me these words were not pleasing to the Lord, and I began correcting myself.

In art class, my paintings took on a spiritual nature, as did my interest in music. I began to write poetry as notes to match the words tumbled through my head. My love for God could not be denied. It so permeated my being that everything I did led me on a deeper search for truth. Each Sunday morning at church, I listened closely to the priest's words, trying to find God's personal message to me. The rituals which were performed during the service and had become a matter of habit to me from repeating them all my life, now took on a different meaning.

As spring approached, I'd begun going into the gym after lunch to be near some of the kids I'd seen wearing the "Jesus People" buttons. I shyly sat down on the creaky bleacher a few feet from a curly haired girl that was very friendly to everyone around her.

"Hey" I said quietly, not even sure she had heard. "Well hey there yourself! I'm Donna." She said turning and grabbing the blond haired boy I'd first seen wearing the Jesus button back in the fall. "And this is Charlie."

"Hey, I've seen you in the halls before. Good to meet ya!" Charlie said. "You're a senior, aren't you?"

"Yeah, I'm getting out of jail this year." I said grinning. "I noticed y'all wearing those 'Jesus People' buttons earlier in the year. Well," I kind of stammered, but forced myself to continue. "I uh, I just asked Jesus into my life."

"Hey that's great! Why don't you come to our youth group meetings that we have Saturday nights at our church?" Donna asked.

"Yeah, we have lots of fun. There are all kinds of things to do; games and stuff after we have prayer and rap session." Charlie added.

"That sounds good to me. Maybe I can get off work in time Saturday and I'll meet you there." I said. I was glad to be included with some kids around my age that believed in the Lord. I had never belonged to any sort of Christian youth group. For that matter, I'd never even been invited to any youth activities at all even within my own church, so this invitation was surely a welcome change in my life! They all spoke that interesting 'Jesus' lingo that I'd been reading in different books.

That Saturday at work, I was informed by my boss that I'd be working until 9:00, and the schedule change was to include every Saturday for the near future. That announcement abruptly put an end to my hopes of joining a youth group.

Even with this damper, I'd recently been introduced to a very pretty girl with long brown hair and huge brown eyes. Her name was Marlene. Every day during lunch period I looked forward to sitting by her and having light hearted conversations.

As I slid my lunch tray on the table opposite of Marlene, she smiled up at me.

"Hey David, where have you been?" She asked as she nibbled a French Fry.

"Teacher kept us a few minutes late to finish a pop quiz." I added. My heart was beating faster than usual and I was certain that she must be able to hear it. I had been practicing all night in the mirror how to ask her to the prom. It was now or never as the date loomed ever nearer.

"Hey Marlene . . . uh . . ." I stammered.

"Hey there Dave . . . I thought we went through all of that." She snickered slapping me on the hand.

"I know, well, what I mean to say is, you think you might want to go to the prom with me?" There, it was out now! No taking it back!

"Well, I would, but, well, I'm sort of not allowed to date yet. But I would if I were allowed to!" Marlene added quickly, obviously not wanting to hurt my feelings.

"Oh, ok, well in that case, do you want your jello?" I asked smiling.

"No, go ahead and eat it." She laughed.

Even though I was completely crushed at not being able to take Marlene to prom, I was glad that we could still be friends. Our talks about the Lord and other topics were always so inspiring to me and helped me more than she could know.

Time was ticking and the thought of leaving high school forever gave me a queasy feeling down deep inside. I just wasn't sure what I was going to do with my life. I didn't have anyone to turn to for guidance, but I'd decided on my own that I would enroll in the local junior college and try taking courses in between working so I could afford the tuition. Anxiety overwhelmed me at times, but I forced the feelings down in order to be able show a sense of self-confidence around family and friends. The headaches I'd had occasionally now seemed to come with more regularity, although aspirins offered some relief. Only the Lord knew the emotions and turmoil I felt on the inside. I comforted myself with the knowledge that many of my classmates would be going to the same college, so life after high school would indeed be possible.

Graduation parties were being held and I had received a few invitations to some. However when I'd been told that drinking would be involved, I declined, knowing instinctively that I shouldn't take part. Still, hanging around with friends after the ceremony would have been nice, and the thought of nothing to do at graduation brought intense loneliness to my soul.

Graduation day came and there was a small get together at my house consisting of my parents, my younger sister Cathy, my older married sister Cherie and her two-year-old daughter, Mary, and my older married brother Ronnie. Neither my brother nor sister brought their spouses. My Aunt and Uncle came by and had a slice of cake and cup of coffee. I was glad to receive my exquisitely expensive wrist watch as a graduation gift and showed it proudly to everyone in the coming weeks. In spite of the small gathering, I found myself enjoying the little party. However, the next morning would be just another day and time to go to work at the good ole store again.

One night after both my father and Cathy had gone to bed, my mother turned to me during a commercial break with a curious look on her face.

"Dave, I have to ask you something. I've been hearing about something called being 'born-again' at work. Do you know anything about that?" She asked sipping her coffee.

"Yeah. I've been reading the Bible and talking to friends about it and, well, as a matter of fact, I'm born again too!" I added quickly, greatly surprised to hear my mother using this same lingo.

"You are! Well so am I! I said the prayer of salvation just today!" My mother said beaming at me.

We spoke quietly, using all the new terms that we both had recently learned, as though we'd been using them all our lives. We decided it would be best, however to keep this salvation news just between us for the time being.

Neither of us knew at the time that an event was about to take place in just a few short weeks that would turn our world upside and change our lives forever!

CHAPTER 2

THE HOUSE OF PRAISE

To everything there is a season,
And a time to every purpose under the heaven Ecclesiastes 3:1

My mouth formed the words to the popular tune with similar words as it floated through my room. This 'Jesus' movement must be on fire right now! Songs about Jesus were everywhere!

"Davie boy, time for supper." I heard my mother call out. That was all I needed to hear. My favorite meal of southern fried chicken was being prepared tonight. The intoxicating aroma filled the house as my mouth watered, dreaming of a plate full of all my favorites, fried chicken, mashed potatoes and gravy, biscuits and sweet potato pie!

I made it into the kitchen from my room in record speed, even though it was only about ten steps in reality. Sitting down in my corner of the brightly lit little kitchen, Mama motioned for me to come over by the stove. I could tell she had a secret of some sort.

She spoke in quick hushed tones.

"Say Dave, I was talking to Flora-May at work today, you know a Christian girl that's kind of, well, you know, on the beefy side, but nice, real nice? Anyway, we talk about the Lord and she was telling me about this place that has sort of prayer meetings or something like that. They're held on Sunday nights at a farm out in the country and she say's she really enjoys 'em. Maybe you ought to go, and see, huh?" She asked.

"Well yeah, but how do I know where it is or how to get there?" I asked, my shyness having made me a bit anxious at the thought of a room full of strangers, but my enthusiasm for my newfound faith pressing me forward.

"Now Flora-May already told me she'd come and get you." Mama said encouraging me along.

"Oh Mama, Flora-May! I answered frowning in dismay. Mama had described her with great glee many times in the past. I could just hear her: "Now bless her heart, that Flora-May's back side's as big as a barn". The thought of it scared me half to death! As everyone in the south knew, it was the kiss of death to get the B.H.H.! That was either 'bless her heart or bless his heart; always to be followed by something that in any other state north of the Mason Dixon line would be unabridged gossip. But down south, it was known that you could pretty much say anything using the B.H.H. rule and it always came out as acceptable in polite company.

"Don't be silly David; she's a perfectly nice young Christian girl. God don't care none about looks and neither should we. Besides, when she wears black with a long tunic top, you hardly notice that giant caboose of hers." Mama couldn't resist adding in that last little tidbit, which tortured me further. "She's just as cute as a little red wagon! You'll see!"

"Oohhh, ok then. I don't see as how I have much of a choice anyway." I answered slowly. I was understandably quite hesitant about the whole thing. But still, she was a 'born-again' Christian and I was anxious to get to know any and all of them that I could find!

The following Sunday morning, as I was driving toward St. Thomas for the 11:00 mass, I glanced across the highway and noticed the ocean looked as though diamonds were dancing on the water in the brilliant sunlight. "Does everything look more beautiful after you have been "born again"? I asked the Lord. It did seem the ocean breeze smelled sweeter, the old oaks that draped the scenic beach highway seemed more majestic and the music sung by the youth choir, more uplifting than ever before.

As the usual Sunday morning service began, the leader of the youth choir asked the audience to join in on one of my favorite songs which had been added recently to their repertoire.

I am the resurrection and the life; He who believes in me will never die . . .

The haunting melody based on a scripture was played in a minor key. The guitar's smooth rhythmic patterns together with the steady beat of the tambourine, and the harmonious singing of the teenagers compelled one and all to join in the worshipful song.

Eleven O'clock church services had always been geared towards the young people. The service continued with the usual readings by the priest and audience responses written in our prayer books. Almost everyone was thoroughly familiar with the weekly prayers and worship. Soon, the time came for communion. The youth choir sang an appropriate song quietly in the background as the congregation lined up to go to the front and be administered the sacrament. Soon, the priest was giving the benediction and I was quickly out the door and headed for home. The service was somehow more meaningful to me than it had been in the past, I thought as I made the short mile and a half drive home.

The afternoon flew by and I found myself waiting outside on the little screened in porch my father had added onto our small wooden house. I watched each and every car that went past, hoping it would be my ride to "the House of Praise", as my mother had said this place was called.

"Dave, you want a cup of hot coffee?" Mama asked me through the screen door. She already had showered and was wearing her faded yellow cotton housecoat, ready to relax for the evening.

"Sure sounds good Mama, thanks." I added. I watched her walk through the door as she came with a cup of coffee in both hands. "Ah mercy me" she said as she settled into her old wooden Dedeaux rocker. It was made by a family of Cajuns that had their own business making solid oak rockers. In our neck of the woods, you had really "arrived" when you were the proud owner of a rocking chair stamped "made by the Dedeaux Clan". It was a mark of southern living at its finest, right along side a cup of real southern seafood gumbo or a deep fried oyster po-boy; "fully dressed"; the only way to order one of the devastatingly delicious sandwiches made exclusively in the southern blue-collar coastal areas.

I only managed to take a few sips of my coffee before Flora May rolled up in her "woody", a 1960's style station wagon with most of the wood missing on the driver's side. It creaked as it went over the hump in our driveway.

"Hey Miss Ider" Flora May hung her hand out of the window waving to Mama.

"Flora May" Mama said with a nod and a wave. "Y'all have a real good time tonight now ya hear?"

"Yes Ma'am! I'll see you at work tomorrow!" Flora May called out. "Get in anywhere you can squeeze yourself into." She called out happily. There were two other women in the car, even though at first glance, it seemed like more. Flora May took up most of the front seat, but in what room was left, was a woman around the age of my mom, rather plain but with a kind expression. Flora May introduced her to me as "Sister Parker". I assumed she must be a nun out of her habit. Nuns were quite a bit less formal these days, so it didn't strike me as odd.

"Hey, I'm Cindy, Flora May's cousin" the girl in the back seat next to me introduced herself. She was heavy-set, although comparatively thin to her older cousin, Flora May. Her hair was thick and wavy, touching her shoulders. Her face was round and smiling with tiny eyes set close together.

"Hey" I croaked out, my voice quieter than I intended. "Oh praise the Lord, he's shy Cindy, now don't go a scarin' him to pieces!" Flora May teased before erupting in peals of laughter.

Flora May reached over, turning on the radio and adjusting the knob to my favorite station situated close to the left end of the AM radio dial.

"Wow! The mighty 690!" the station disc jockey crowed. "Yee Haw! 690!" Flora May bellowed. I was beginning to see why Mama liked this fun loving woman so much. She was a cut up and loads of fun to be around!

Just then I noticed a disapproving look being shot over at Flora May from Sister Parker. The raucous disc jockey must have offended her. Flora May quietly reached over and switched the radio off.

"Oh Sister Parker" Cindy spoke up. "I almost forgot to tell you! Praise the Lord, I got that job interview we've been praying about!" Cindy declared happily.

"Oh thank you Jesus!" Sister Parker said joyously. "Now isn't our God good?"

"Hallelujah!" Cindy and Flora May interjected.

The conversation flowed easily between everyone and was so peppered with Thank you Jesus', Praise the Lord's and Hallelujah's that I nearly slipped and added them into my own speech a few times!

The old woody twisted and turned through roads I'd never been down before. The countryside was lovely as the sun began to set, casting its rich purple and dusky gray hues across the sky and over the tops of the giant old oak trees. I could barely make out the words on a simply carved wooden sign that hung beneath a moss-strewn oak as we turned into the pebble driveway that read:

The House of Praise, where Jesus is Lord

The long driveway was flanked by old magnolia trees encircled with azalea bushes. The old farmhouse at the end of the drive was white with green shutters and a porch that wrapped around from front to back, with a wooden swing hanging on the end; giving it a welcoming aura.

"Well Sister Parker and Sister Cindy, come in, come in!" A friendly man greeted us as we came through the old back service porch into an open room with dark wood floors and antique furniture. People were milling about, hugging one another as though they had not seen each other in a great long time.

"This is Brother David" I was introduced.

"Hmm, maybe she's not a nun then because everyone is either sister or brother here, including me!" I thought to myself.

They had 'warned' me on the way over that I might be a bit shocked at what would transpire in the evening worship service. That was more than fine with me. I was ready for something different to shake up my somewhat monotonous routine. I was wide open for anything and anxious to taste a new life in the Lord!

There were about fifty to sixty people milling about the large, brightly lit room. Candles glowed from every corner. The dress of the people was casual and ranged from blue jeans to long, swishing skirts worn by some of the young women.

"Oh hey, Sister Lynne and Sister Kathy! This is brother Dave from Long Beach" sister Parker announced to the two pretty, young women who were actually blood sisters, but looked nothing alike, yet complimented one another perfectly. Lynne had straight jet-black hair that fell past her hips. She wore large framed glasses which accented her huge brown eyes and pretty smile. Her younger sister, Kathy, had waist length chestnut brown hair and an angelically sweet face which seemed to be lit from within as she extended her dainty hand to greet me. Both girls sat on the floor with grace and ease, crossing their legs and tucking them beneath them, their maxi skirts gathered gently about them as someone started to lead the group in a chorus.

> "Clap your hands, all ye people, shout unto God with a voice of triumph!
> (Based on Psalm 47:1)

Joyful shouts of praise to the Lord could be heard from every corner of the room: "Praise you Jesus"; "Thank you Lord"; "I worship your name Lord".

These songs from the Psalms continued in carefree and blissful worship from the young men and women in the room. I was in rapt attention and noticed everyone, including many airmen who were stationed at the local base in Biloxi. The mood turned more reverent when the next song that evolved was a slow and worshipful tune:

> "Seek ye first the kingdom of God, and His righteousness; and all these things shall be added unto you, (Based on Matthew 6:33)

The haunting melody was being sung in harmony with a lovely soprano voice weaving her tune like a nightingale whose notes reached upward to heaven itself. I gazed with wonder at everyone in the room whose eyes were closed and hands were raised in a dream like state. Then, as if by magic, everyone in the room began to sing their own personal praises to the Lord. Eerily they somehow miraculously blended together in the most beautiful, ethereal music my ears had ever heard. The chant vocalized into a crescendo then decrescendo until it grew quiet as a whisper and stopped all at once.

A young man with carrot red hair wearing bib overalls stood up and began to speak in some foreign tongue of which I had never heard, then sat down, his eyes still closed. The room whispered words of praise until another young man, with dark hair wearing a military uniform stood up and began to speak as though the Lord God Himself was speaking directly through him to everyone in the room.

"My children look not to the right, nor to the left, but follow Me and I will lead you to the straight and narrow path!"

A chill ran up my spine as everyone in the room raised their hands once more in thankfulness to the Lord for His words to them on this special and sacred night. Could this be real? Could I be witnessing a true miracle and if so, why had I never seen anything like this before in my life?

Just then a man of medium build and trim brown hair stood up to the podium and opened his Bible. There was a hushed excitement by all as they turned to this man with rapt attention, waiting to hear the word of the Lord from the enlightened leader.

The man spoke with conviction and passion. His fervor for the word of God was both persuasive and exhilarating, stirring me from deep within. I knew without a doubt in my mind that I'd found what I'd been looking for. I would be back just as soon as they had another meeting! These people all resembled the picture I had drawn in my mind of what the 'Jesus People' would look like.

After the meeting drew to a close, people milled about and introduced themselves to me, happy to have me at "The House of Praise". I knew I would never remember all of them, yet some stood out in my mind for various reasons, such as Brother Larry and Brother Dean. They were both airmen and had a pleasant casual air about them that made me hopeful we could become friends in Christ since I planned on coming here as often as possible.

I even met several people who had a similar religious background as I did, but they were joking about the rituals from their former churches, which both gave me pause, and made me feel as though someone understood where I was coming from. Maybe all the traditions I had learned really were nothing more than man made dogma. I was ready to shed like a skin anything that might not be "of the Lord". I also met the speaker for the night. His name was Brother Wendall.

I noticed a kindly looking black woman who later was introduced to me as Sister Tate. She looked vaguely familiar, but I couldn't quite put my finger on it. Oh well. I would probably see her again at the Farm and figure it all out later.

I overheard a short conversation in which Sister Parker was referred to as the "Long Beach emissary." I didn't quite understand the meaning of that, but then there were so many new terms floating around tonight that I had never heard. I decided then and there that I would commit these to memory and learn as much as possible!

As we strolled down the long drive to Flora May's car, the stars seemed to sparkle brighter than I'd ever seen before.

"Hope we didn't scare you too badly tonight" Sister Parker said smiling.

"Oh, well, no, of course not! I loved it! In fact, if it's ok with everyone, I'd really like to start coming here every Sunday night!" I said, hoping they would accept me into this new and exciting worship circle.

"That would be wonderful Brother Dave. There are some home study courses, right in Long Beach at my house as a matter of fact, if you'd like to attend. They're held Tuesday's around lunch time and again on Sunday mornings." Sister Parker answered with a broad smile.

That was it! I was in! A thousand questions swirled through my mind as I began to ask about the things that puzzled me during the service.

"What was that beautiful singing where no one was leading and everyone sang a different tune?" I asked openly.

"Oh that was the high praises. It's the highest form of worship we can give to the Lord." Cindy answered in a singsong voice.

"Well what about that red-headed fellow; was he speaking in tongues? I've read about that in some of my new books." I asked, hoping I didn't sound too ignorant of what I obviously should have known.

They patiently answered each of my questions and commented that I seemed very hungry for the Lord. I felt as though I had learned more in this one night than I had in all my life at regular church services!

The long ride home seemed to fly by in mere moments as we pulled up into my driveway. I glanced at my watch which read 11:30. Oh my goodness, my folks will just never in a million years understand how I could stay at a church service for this long! I'll have to tip toe in tonight and hope they don't notice the time!

That night my head swirled with the happy, worshipful images of the faces and events I'd witnessed at the Farm. The coming week passed quickly, albeit quite mundanely as I lived for Sunday night and going to another service!

I decided to effect some changes in my personal life. Without going off the deep end, so to speak, I'd take one step at a time towards separating from the world. I stopped listening to quite as much of the upbeat music and instead bought a couple of good soft rock tapes. Some of the lyrics even began to remind me of God as I would hum along to the tunes.

I remembered when I was only 11 years old and had taken a few piano lessons. I learned quickly and was performing at school recitals before I knew it. Once when I was practicing at home on a warm spring day with the door open, I was concentrating on playing a particularly difficult classical piece. When I finished playing, I heard applause coming from outside the screen door. I was shocked to find about five neighborhood boys assembled there, certainly *not* the classical music listening kind of kids, but there they were none the less, clapping, for *me*!

"I had no idea you could play like that Dave!" One boy with a dirty baseball cap said.

"Yeah Woods, you been holding out on us, man!" another boy with a ragged t-shirt and holey blue jeans shot out.

Now it may not have been a review in a big newspaper, but it was like receiving an award to me. I'd never before had such encouragement from anyone about anything, especially about my piano playing! However,

I became distracted later on, as most eleven year olds will be. Having lost all interest in practicing, I soon made the decision to quit my lessons for a while. Weeks turned into months as the old upright piano gathered dust in the corner. After a few years, my parents gave up hope that I would return to playing, so they put an ad in the paper and sold the instrument.

But now, the desire to play the piano had once again taken root in my heart. I decided to discuss this with my Dad since he was a musician himself.

"Now son, if you want to buy another piano, you need to take me with you. I'm more experienced with those shysters trying to make a sale. Your old Daddy will see to it you don't get cheated!" He pronounced proudly.

Now it was a well-known fact within our household that Daddy was *the* man and when it came to horse trading of any sort, he was a master! He had bought and sold more cars, trucks, boats, motorcycles and the like than possibly any human being on the planet. He almost seemed to live for it! It was his chosen sport! I had saved up enough to buy a second hand piano and at the end of a day of my father dickering around on various price lowering strategies, I came home as the proud owner of a used upright spinet piano! Ta Da!

I thought about acquiring lessons, but decided to hold off. Maybe if I got 'Spirit filled' the Lord would lead me and teach me to play for Him without all that hard work.

The week flew by and before I knew it, I was clocking out of work on a Saturday night. I had planned on going to mass at St. Thomas this evening, but because of a few overtime hours, those plans had to be scrapped.

Bright and early Sunday morning, I was up and showered, having a cup of coffee and toast with my Mom before heading over to Sister Parker's home for Bible study.

"Oh I wish I could go!" Mama said crunching on her toast. She could speak freely because Daddy was in his shop tinkering with something for the new boat he'd recently bought.

"I never much liked St. Thomas anyway. I like a good preachin' that makes you *feel* like you've been to church! You know, where the preacher pounds his fist and the folks yell 'Amen!'" "Mama took a long swig of her coffee as she contemplated more. "I need to work on your Daddy some."

26

"Well don't do it when I'm around, if you please!" I answered. Taking my last bite of toast I slipped out the screened door and was in my car almost before I heard the slapping of the screen door as it clapped against its wood frame. "Bye Mama."

"Bye hon. See you for lunch, huh?" Mama asked.

"Yes Ma'am." I said as I eased my car down the drive way and into the street, carefully avoiding the potholes.

Sister Parker's house was only about a half mile from our house and sat perched on a quiet street corner. The tiny white clapboard home looked friendly, albeit worn and in need of a good paint job at the least.

"Why Brother Dave, come right on in here, Praise the Lord! Were just so glad you could make it this morning, thank you Jesus!" Sister Parker said smiling and gently guiding me into her living room, which was even smaller than my parent's house, and was already filling up with 'Jesus people'.

"Brother Dave, this is sister Dolly." Sister Parker introduced me to the kind looking lady with bright red hair brushed high upon her head in a bee-hive fashion.

"Why praise the Lord brother Dave, I've heard so much about you! I'm just glad that everyone hasn't scared you off!" Sister Dolly said with a distinct Pennsylvania Dutch accent, which was quite similar to Brother Wendell's, the man who had preached last Sunday night.

"You know I have a son, Paul, who is close to your age I'd love for you to meet!" Sister Dolly continued brightly. "He's been to the House of Praise once, but that was quite some time back. I think all he needs is just a little encouragement from someone like you and he would join in. Praise the Lord for sending you here Brother Dave, because I think my son Paul just might be a mission that the Lord is sending you on." Sister Dolly said, her dark brown eyes were quite sincere and this somehow made me feel more a part of the group.

"Sister Parker, what is that you're cooking? It smells heavenly!" Sister Dolly said turning her head to see Sister Parker stirring something on the old white gas stove, the knobs well worn porcelain cracking from years of heat and heavy use.

"Oh just some lunch I'm throwing together. We'd best get the lesson started before the time gets away from us." Sister Parker added putting down the large wooden spoon onto the speckled black and white lid.

"Ok, well, once again, I must explain to you that although I'm a woman teaching this class," she said softly and clearing her throat; "I will assure you that I am under the cover of my husband, even though he is not present at this time. Also, Brother Wendall has given me his blessing to teach, so I'm in accordance with the word and in submission to both my husband and our shepherd."

"Well everyone has only the utmost respect for this preacher, Brother Wendall. He must be walking mighty close with the Lord." I thought to myself as Sister Parker opened her well-worn black Bible to begin the lesson. After a simple prayer of blessing the teaching began. Just then the door opened and Cindy entered holding a tissue and sniffling.

"Oh Praise the Lord, I'm so sorry to be late everyone! I have the symptoms of a cold" Cindy said as she raised one hand in victory and praise to the Lord, "but bless God I know I'm healed because I prayed and asked Jesus to heal me! But Satan is seeing to it that I have the symptoms to fight with. Aaaaa-chew!"

"Well praise God! Oh these young Christians are learning so fast! Why it took me over a year to have that kind of faith!" Sister Dolly remarked kindly. "I don't know if I have that much still." She said smiling. She had a way about her that made you feel special just by the way she spoke to you. I couldn't help but feel a warm fondness for this kindly woman. I hoped I would meet her son, Paul soon. If he was anything like his mother I had no doubt we would become fast friends.

The teaching was very interesting and I heard things that I'd never heard before. Now I was even more certain that I had found God's holy truth for the first time in my life.

After about an hour, the meeting ended with a prayer. Everyone's arms were uplifted to the heavens with soft whispers of "thank you Jesus" resounding throughout the tiny room. I was included in the conversations afterward and we even exchanged phone numbers. Later that afternoon I was delighted when Sister Parker called and asked if I could pick up sister Dolly for the evenings services at the Farm. She told me she would not be able to go and that Sister Dolly and her son Paul would be in need of a ride. After getting the directions to their home, which was only about two miles from my house, I set out the door to go and pick up my new friends in the Lord. The excitement welled up within me for yet another night of worship and learning. I also was excited to be meeting sister Dolly's son, Paul for the first time!

As I pulled into the driveway of sister Dolly's small brick home, I thought to myself how nice it looked. The subdivision was newly built, compared to mine, but I hardly gave it a second thought. I was content with the home I'd lived in since I was five years old and its familiarity was both warm and comfortable.

Sister Cindy was at the door waving me in. "Come on in Brother David! We've been waiting for you!" Cindy introduced me to Paul, a young man only about a year older than my sister Cathy, but he looked older. He had blond curly hair and a mustache. He wore brown corduroy pants with a Woodstock t-shirt.

"Hey man." Paul said as I shook his hand.

"Hey, I'm glad you're coming with us tonight. Your mom told me about you and I'd hoped to meet you soon." I answered, truly happy that he was joining our little group.

"Well we'd best get going. You know how brother Wendall doesn't like late comers." Sister Dolly said picking up her purse and patting her giant red beehive.

I felt as though I'd known Paul for years. We fell into an automatic friendship and the conversation flowed freely between the four of us. Cindy seemed especially cheerful and in high spirits talking to both Paul and I the entire ride.

As we walked into the large receiving room that was the place of worship, I already felt as though the things in the room were becoming familiar to me. There were greetings of "Hello Brother Dave! Glad to have you back with us tonight, praise the Lord!" from folks I'd met last week. The room was filled with electricity as we settled into our places and began the singing for the night.

"Great is the Lord, and greatly to be praised!" Oh good, I remember that one, I thought to myself. These scripture choruses surely were catchy.

As I looked around, everyone in the entire room had their hands raised and their eyes closed as their faces turned upward to God. The candle-lit room bathed each face in a soft golden light, like beams from heaven. The urge to raise my hands became unbearable as I felt my arms reaching toward God, slowly, naturally, gloriously.

"Alleluia!, Alleluia! Thank you Jesus! We worship you Lord!" The sweet notes came from deep within each person, separately, yet jointly, in unison, and altogether harmonious. I found myself joining in as though I'd sung these 'high praises' all my life. The Spirit of God flowed from person to person, as if filling one cup, then overflowing to the next until the entire room was filled to overflowing with the Holy Spirit. This must be what the upper room was like when that holy moment came and the entire place was afire with the Spirit of God. How special and sacred this house must be that God had chosen it and the people within to be touched by His presence. "Oh thank you Jesus!" The words came from my own throat this time, gently and in tune with all the other worshipers. Just as suddenly as the high praises started, they stopped, each person continuing to worship the Lord in a hushed silence as a young man stood up and with a thunderous voice began speaking, and then shouting with tears streaming down his face, in a tongue so strange, yet so lovely, it brought tears to my eyes. Then silence immersed the room once more. I slowly opened my eyes. I could almost hear the candles as the flames flickered in an instant breeze that swept the room, and then another young man stood to his feet:

"Shout with joy unto the Lord for He is worthy of our praises! Worship Him and Him alone, for God is a jealous God. He will reward the just and the upright!" The man slowly sat down and the room once more began its own crescendo into high praises that filled this holy place. The joy that spilled from the hearts of each one present could be felt in an aching, yet sensational vocal crescendo to God Almighty. In my entire life, I'd never felt so completely loved and overflowing with such comfort and acceptance. I was one with these brothers and sisters, forever bound in the joy of the Lord.

A time of testimony then began as person after person rose to tell of opportunities they'd had to witness at work or school. "Amen's and Hallelujah's" followed each testimony.

One rather frightened looking young girl stood up. Her eyes looked as though she'd been crying, but then many had been crying from joy. She held her head high in an effort to bring her emotions under control. "I'd like to ask for prayer tonight. I've been under attack from Satan all week long, and," Just then she was cut off by one of the elders.

"We will handle that afterwards. You may take your seat now." The serious looking man put his hand up and smiled knowingly. "All things in their proper order brothers and sisters."

"Amen!" Thank you Jesus!" resounded through the room. I wasn't really sure what had just happened, but assumed that she had spoken out of turn and the elders didn't want her to spoil the joy of this special night. The service had been flowing according to God's will.

Just then another hush fell over the crowd as brother Wendall took his now familiar position at the podium. After a brief prayer for a blessing upon the words he would now speak, he began with a thunderous voice and upraised hands:

"Praise the Lord God Jehovah, for he is great and greatly to be praised!" His voice boomed across the room with great authority.

"Amen! Hallelujah!" The agreements broke forth throughout the room. I could feel the hair on the back of my neck raise. Surely the presence of God was in this man and speaking through him once more.

Brother Wendall began his sermon using scripture passages from Revelations. The wisdom this man possessed about the coming of the Lord was an astounding and marvelous phenomenon to behold! I'd never learned so much about the return of Jesus as I had in one night! By the end of the service, my mind was made up. There would be no more St. Thomas for me. I was a part of this body of Christ and wanted to tell brother Wendall about my decision.

I made my way through the crowd of people, receiving at least ten hugs from the surrounding people along the way. Brother Wendall was enclosed by people who were speaking with him about tonight's message, trying to glean as much wisdom from him as possible. "Oh Brother David, it's good to see you here again tonight!" Brother Wendall said putting his hand firmly and welcomingly on my shoulder. "How are you enjoying the services?"

"Well, uhm, that's what I wanted to talk to you about. I really just can't believe how wonderful this place is! I've decided that I want to be a regular part of this body of Christ from now on." Gosh I even was beginning to sound like everyone else! I'd picked up the lingo quickly and the words were now becoming a regular part of my vocabulary.

"Well that's great news Brother Dave! But you want to make certain that you do tell your parents and receive their permission. You know you must be in submission to their authority in all things, brother." Brother Wendall said looking deep into my eyes.

"Oh well, of course, yes." I said as though I understood exactly what he meant, although I was utterly confused. I was eighteen now and how on earth did I need my parents' permission? I could even vote without their permission! But be that as it may, I'd find a way to tell my mom first. She'd be all for it!

"Hey Brother Dave, let's go grab a pizza!" Sister Cindy said touching my shoulder from the back seat.

"That's fine by me!" Sister Dolly chimed in along with her son Paul, who now was smiling and carefree; fitting in as though he'd been going to the farm all his life.

The meal and fellowship continued as we each shared things about our daily lives with one another. This fellowship time became a regular tradition on Sunday nights after service and became the focal point of my social life. One night after eating, I couldn't hide a yawn that forced its way out.

"What's wrong brother Dave, are we boring you?" Paul spoke up.

"No no, it's nothing like that. But I will ask for y'all to pray for me. I've just been so exhausted with classes at college during the day, then working all afternoon, then homework and then working all day on Saturday and even some Sunday's. It's just wearing me down. I feel like the Lord might be trying to tell me something." I said holding my head down.

"We will pray right now!" Sister Cindy chimed in and put her hands on my shoulders, praying fervently for God's guidance and help in my life. The prayer ended with each of us having tears in our eyes. I felt God had spoken to me then and there through my brother and sister in Christ. He didn't want me pursuing college anymore. I needed more time and energy to focus on Him and fellowshipping with other believers. I had to choose between the world and the Lord. I chose the Lord!

With my mind made up, I went into the admissions office to inform them of my decision to withdraw from classes. "I'll have to tell the guidance counselor. She'll be right with you." Within moments, I heard the clicking of heels on the hard linoleum school floors. As I looked up, I was greeted by the kind face of Sister Tate, the black woman I'd met at the House of Praise. Then it came to me that Sister Tate was also the same person I'd seen for years at the grocery store. You know a good education is the key to success today and I'm afraid that without it the doors you need to open will be forever locked to you. You have such potential Dave; I just hate to see it wasted. Even though there is nothing wrong with working at a store, it's clear that you could do so much more with your life and your gifts." Sister Tate said passionately.

"No, I've made up mind and I won't turn back. I feel this is what the Lord wants me to do." I answered respectfully.

"Well," she said shaking her head slowly "If this is what you think you have to do, I can't stop you, but please know the doors will be open to you if you should ever want to return." She said with a smile.

I thanked her and felt as though a burden had been lifted from my shoulders when I drove away in my 66 Comet. I would be able to get the rest my body craved and still work my job, which was an obvious requirement, and follow the Lord closer by being part of the new fellowship meetings in a deeper, more committed way. I just couldn't continue to burn the candle at both ends with college and working, even if I had never stepped foot inside the doors of the House of Praise. I'd briefly discussed it with my mother, who never really saw much value of higher education and encouraged me to 'go on and quit.' While my Dad was noticeably less excited about my decision, he reluctantly went along with it as well. However, he did make the suggestion that I think about applying for a job at the Post Office. "If you can get on at a good company at a young age, you don't need college". He had made the proclamation on many occasions.

As the weeks ebbed and flowed with the rhythm of the seasons gently changing to a warm autumn, there were also changes in the company who rode to the House of Praise with me each week. Flora May had never gone with us except for that very first time. Cindy had invited her cousin

Karla along and she had accepted the Lord in the back seat one night after services. Oh what a joyous night that had been! Karla and Cindy looked nothing alike to be cousins. Although they were both quite on the heavy side, Karla had a pretty face and waist length thick brown hair. They both seemed to be very drawn to Paul, but I just felt this was in a friendship type of way. Cindy and Karla became the very closest of friends and began to take their own car to the House of Praise, meeting Paul and I there and then going out to eat afterwards.

My fourteen-year-old sister, Cathy, had begun to show an interest in the Fellowship also. I decided to tape record the high praises for her to listen to, since she was very interested in music and had a beautiful singing voice. She was moved to tears, expressing that she could almost hear the angels singing along with us. I told her that perhaps the angels were indeed present.

She rode with Paul and I one night and quickly joined in the singing with her hands lifted as though she'd been doing it all her life. Her soprano voice blended and enriched the sound as her voice out in praise to God.

That night at the pizza place, I noticed that Cindy and Karla were a bit removed and almost cool acting when I introduced them to Cathy. There were no "Sister Cathy's or Praise the Lord, we're happy you came tonight." But Cathy had been very warmly welcomed by all the brethren who patted me on the shoulder, wanting to meet the new girl. Cathy became a member of my close circle of friends and quickly gave up going to St. Thomas in favor of this new fellowship at the House of Praise.

The cool gray days of November came and were a welcome relief from the oppressive heat of summertime. I found myself drawn to the lunchtime meetings held once a week at Sister Parker's home, at least on those days I wasn't scheduled to work. I was able to learn more about my newfound faith, enriching the overall experience that now consumed my life. Gone were the days of sitting in front of the television set watching such worldly and demonic programs as some of the popular science fiction episodes I used to enjoy. Whenever I was tempted to watch such trash, I now rebuked the devil and retreated to my room where I would learn more of God's word.

CHAPTER 3

DELIVERANCE

"Cindy, I see those cold symptoms have finally gone away." I said greeting my friend as I entered Sister Parker's house for the weekly lunch time Bible study.

"Yeah, the devil finally realized I wasn't going to let him win the battle, Praise the Lord!" Cindy said raising one arm in victory. Neither one of us would acknowledge that a cold usually only lasts a little more than a week anyway.

For some reason, she and I never referred to one another as sister or brother. It was the same way with our new friend Paul. But everyone else remained firmly sisters and brothers in our daily conversations.

"Why Brother David, Sister Cindy, bless God, good to see you here! Oh my, are you ever going to be hearing some prophecy today! This is really only for the more mature Christians in the Lord, so we share this at special meetings. That's why the elders and I are all here today!" Brother Wendall said in hushed tones.

I could see the elders all around the dining room table. None of them were over the age of twenty-five.

"Oh praise the Lord, how exciting!" Cindy said; her eyes twinkling as she looked towards the young elders, all of whom were single, *and* male.

"Prophecy? I'm really interested in learning and hearing all about God's word!" I said expecting to hear words of encouragement, once more uplifting our spirits into high praises for the King of Kings.

"This will be like no teaching you have ever heard, that's for certain! It will be inspired from Revelations! God has been speaking to me about the things that are to come and admonishing me that I'm to teach the brethren how to survive the coming times of heavy trials. It's coming you know, brother Dave, and we must know that much suffering and sacrifice are ahead for the true believers. All of the 'carnal-Christians' will fall away as the word says when the seeds are planted in shallow ground. The weeds come and choke them out, crushing them! We must be planted deep to survive!" Brother Wendall said with his Pennsylvanian accent as he pummeled his fist into his hand.

"Oh, um, yes." I said quietly, my heart catching in my throat. This wasn't exactly what I had in mind.

The adults and "more mature Christians" were all a buzz; speaking knowledgeably using terms such as "rapture", "the great tribulation" and also about the trials and valleys we would all be going through as a result of the end times we were most assuredly already living in.

"Dave, ppssst!" Cindy said taking me by the elbow and leading me to a quiet corner before the meeting began.

"You see that woman over there at the table with the snow white hair?" Cindy said nodding in the direction of a mysterious looking woman who seemed to be staring straight through any and all who came near her. She was thin and probably in her early sixties. I could see clearly her hard, square face, suntanned like leather, accentuating her blue eyes. These eyes were not a soft sky blue, but more of a steely blue, which seemed to pierce any who came too near the harsh glare.

36

"Yeah, kind of scary, huh?" I whispered.

"You don't know just how scary she *really* is! That's Sister Miriam! Everyone has to pass the 'Miriam' test, so I'm just giving you fair warning. "Cindy said trying not to be too conspicuous.

"What in the world is the 'Miriam' test? It sounds painful!" I could feel my heart begin to race at the thought.

"Well, you're gonna find out soon enough, so I might as well tell you. She has the gift of discernment. She can see if you have any demons! Also, if you can remain humble in her presence, you have passed! She has a way of 'getting your goat' though. Come on, the meeting's gonna start. I can't say anymore right now." Cindy said walking casually over to the table.

While the prospect of being "discerned" by this severe looking woman with the ruthless glare frightened me, the urge to gain more knowledge of the times that were to come pushed me forward. I hoped the fear didn't show on my face.

"You know I think any one of our top political leaders could very well be the anti-Christ" Sister Miriam added, casting a glance in my direction.

"No, no sister, let's not make any hasty judgments. However, the anti-Christ is surely out there, alive and well and just waiting for his time to come." Brother Wendall added.

"That's right! All the signs from the both the Old Testament and the New have lined up. The foolish ones in the regular Sunday-go-to-meeting churches are going to miss it! They are so deceived and blind, singing their hymns and thinking they are on the true path. The time is coming when everyone is going to choose or be doomed into becoming the devil's servant!" Brother Andy piped up.

The fear I had regarding these "end time prophecies" somehow got mixed up in my mind with all of the other fears I'd tucked away through the years. I was still of prime drafting age. The memories of the recent Vietnam War haunted me as well.

This war that brother Wendall and the others spoke of sounded like nothing less than Armageddon! The end of all time! I still had life to experience, a wife, a family, even grandchildren. Would I ever be able to enjoy any of these things? The thought of fighting in a battle brought images of the worst sort of pain and suffering on not just me, but thousands of others. I never had the capacity to see anything suffer, not even a sparrow.

I tried asking a few questions, but they all sounded imprudent. I decided that it was unwise to ask anything further until I had studied the Bible, and in particular, Revelations in greater depth!

Anxiety began to build in my chest. My face must have been strawberry red the way my heart was pounding. I had to make myself stop fidgeting. I needed to appear much more casual to seem as though I were just as wise and spiritual as everyone else in the room. Why is it that these other Christians don't have any sense of dread about them? I would *have* to grow and mature in the Lord and I *would* do so!

Just then, Sister Miriam looked my way. I could feel her icy cold stare go all through me. I felt myself fidgeting once more; fingering the long hair from my forehead.

"Excuse me for interrupting, brother Wendall. I don't want to be out of order here." Sister Miriam spoke out raising her claw like hand.

"No sister Miriam, go right ahead. I sanction your wisdom in this meeting." Brother Wendall said solemnly.

"Brother Dave, I feel that you have a need to rebuke Satan." Sister Miriam said, her voice beginning to rise as her eyes widened. "He's all over you right now, casting a spirit of fear about you and into this entire room!" Her voice boomed as each word became louder and higher pitched.

The whole group of people reached their hands towards me. Those close enough to me were touching me about my shoulders and head and then with outstretched hands, all began to chant, "Praise you Jesus! We rebuke you Satan in the name of Jesus! Satan, go back to the pit of hell from whence you came!"

I bowed my head and joined in the chant. Just as quickly as the praying started, it ceased. I looked up and could see Sister Miriam's piercing blue eyes boring directly into me, causing me wince instinctively.

"Brother Wendall, I think we have some cleaning up to do with this one." Sister Miriam said looking as though she were ready to take control and handle this 'situation' immediately!

Sister Parker gently placed her hand on Sister Miriam's thin, brown arm. The message was clear from the look on her face as she conveyed it. I was not yet ready for these deep truths. It wasn't time . . . . yet.

I had no idea what this "cleaning up" was and I'll confess I was in no great hurry to find out anytime soon!

"Well brethren, I can smell sister Parker's luncheon meal, so I'd do well to have all things in order and close our meeting so we can enjoy fellowship and breaking of bread together, Amen!" Brother Wendall said smiling, rocking back and forth in his chair, like a child who was a bit too anxious to be fed.

"Sister, Parker, bless the Lord, I haven't had a meal this good in years! It reminds me of the cooking I had back in Pennsylvania! You know Sister; you should be sharing your wisdom with the younger sisters in our group so they will be able to be prudent wives when the hard times come. No one knows any longer how to survive! They think they just go to the grocery store and buy a box of cereal. Well what happens when there are no stores, no corner burger joints to serve your every need? People need to learn how to farm and cook and preserve foods!" Brother Wendall said as he slurped the last drops of soup from his bowl.

"It blesses my soul to feed my shepherd." Sister Parker said as she immediately refilled his empty bowl with more steaming hot soup. "I'll be happy to pass on my knowledge to the younger sisters in the Lord." Sister Parker said with a humble smile.

I cringed at the thought of not having a hamburger and fries from the local fast food place once in awhile. Are things really going to be this bad? I would have to somehow learn to deal with the losses of modern conveniences I'd taken for granted for so long. However, I could not see myself learning the skills of farming any time soon. In my mind, vegetables grew in the produce department of the grocery store.

In the months that followed, I continued growing in the Lord and learning all that I could. I absorbed everything like a sponge from my new "family" in Christ. At the Tuesday evening gatherings at the House of Praise, it was the practice to divide into groups, rather like a Sunday school situation, and go into different rooms to be taught by the elders. On one particular night, my classroom had a teacher that was not from our fellowship. Nearly the entire lesson was a message consisting of the evils possibly found in the more worldly and incorrect translations of the Bible that were corrosive to the soul and would fill one with the vile of the world if he wasn't careful. According to this guest speaker, the only version that was "true" was the King James.

Seated on a chair by the wall, I felt as though every eye in the classroom could see my paperback Bible. I slid my hand over the avocado green cover with pictures of young people smiling happily and huge letters boasting of the modern English across the cover. I determined then and there that I would buy a King James so that I could be learning God's word correctly. A regular member of the Bible study also noted that every Christian would benefit from a boxed set that he referred to as an "anti-Satan kit" to ward off the wiles of the devil who was always and forever seeking to find a way to infiltrate the realm of the mind and take over your very soul. I made a note of it with the purpose of asking about this kit at the local bookstore.

"Sister Parker, I need to talk to you about something that was said tonight." I mentioned as soon as she, Cindy and I got into the car to head home.

"Do you think that the man who was teaching tonight is, as everyone puts it 'right on', with God's word? I mean some folks have been talking about an anti-Satan kit and warning us that the devil is always trying to take over our minds. The man, whatever his name was, warned us that the King James was the only Bible to read." I asked.

"Well, I'll say this much. Sometimes there are wolves in sheep's clothing, Dave. You need to ask the Lord to show you who your shepherd is supposed to be so that you can go and share these things with him and receive guidance." Sister Parker said.

"Oh Sister Parker, that reminds me. I have something wonderful to share with you!" Cindy piped up. "The Lord told me that Brother Walter is to be my shepherd!" She proclaimed happily.

"Well praise the Lord, child! I was wondering when you were going to figure that one out." Sister Parker replied knowingly.

"Sister Parker! You knew?" Cindy asked.

"Yes, the Lord showed me this some time ago." Sister Parker added patting Cindy on the shoulder.

"The Lord will reveal these truths to us as we are able to see them. But we have to be open to His will at all times and be ready to receive." Sister Parker added.

"But Sister, I've read Psalm 23 and it said that the Lord is our shepherd." I spoke up, unable to keep my concern about having a shepherd to myself.

"Brother Dave, you are still young in the Lord and have so much growing to do. You have to understand that the Lord always refers to His children as sheep. The reason is because sheep are basically stupid animals and must have someone to follow. The Lord created us in this way, so that when we are under our shepherd's protection, we are safe and not in danger of the wiles of the devil, who is like the wolf, always seeking to devour and destroy God's children!" Sister Parker said knowingly.

"Oh I do hope mine is brother Wendall!" I added, secretly worried that it might not be.

"Well we will be in prayer about it for you, so that you will be able to hear God's voice in this matter." Sister Parker said.

Sister Parker and Cindy exchanged a knowing glance and small smile between one another. They always seemed to be privy to the Lord's will and to be able to hear His voice, giving them a secret knowledge that I never quite seemed to grasp.

Life continued in a blur of working, coming home to shower, eat, and leave for meetings, prayer groups and fellowships. Cathy came to the meetings with me when she wasn't attending school. She loved the services and quite naturally seemed to fit right in, especially with all the young men in attendance.

One Sunday night, Cindy came with Paul to pick me up for services at the fellowship. Cathy and I were all ready and sitting on the front porch waiting for her to pull up.

"Here's Cindy and Paul, David. Let me go grab my purse inside real quick." Cathy said excitedly.

"Ok, but hurry. We don't want to be late." I said as the screen door slammed behind me.

"Hey man, get in!" Paul called out.

"Good to see you again!" I said jumping into the back seat.

"Cathy there's no room for you this time!" Cindy called out the window loudly as Cathy walked out the front door.

"What did you say?" Cathy called back with a smile.

"I *said* there's no room for you!" Cindy said loudly once more.

"Oh, um, well, ok. Alright, bye then. Have a good time." Cathy said, still smiling as we pulled out of the driveway.

There seemed to be plenty of room in the back seat I thought to myself. Maybe Cindy's picking someone else up tonight. That's it. No big deal. Cathy can just come next Sunday. She'll understand. If not, I'll start taking my own car each week.

As we drove towards D'Iberville, I began to realize that Cindy wasn't picking anyone else up tonight for the meeting. It seemed odd that she would tell Cathy there was no room for her. Cathy very much liked Cindy and they always hugged whenever they greeted one another. Paul and Cathy had formed a very good friendship, even starting a Campus Crusade for Christ prayer group at their high school. In fact, Paul certainly seemed to favor Cathy's company over Cindy's, so it wasn't that Cathy didn't get along well with everyone. I just couldn't imagine why Cindy would intentionally leave her out of our group.

I didn't have time to ponder the issue that night. Services were particularly intense. The message of the time of Christ's return dominated the evening as brother Wendall passionately spoke, causing conviction from deep inside each person within earshot.

After the service concluded, I was enjoying fellowshipping with the various members of our "flock." Susan, a very pretty young woman with long black hair, and wearing a flowered maxi skirt and long white shawl over her sweater top came my way.

"Why, hey there Brother Dave! Praise the Lord it's so good to see you!" She said giving me a hug.

"Good to see you too Sister Susan, I missed you last Sunday night. Where were you?" I asked, when just then from the floor above me came a loud CLANK, CLANK CLANK, a most annoying sound which Susan completely ignored.

"Oh I went and visited with our brethren at a church in Louisiana! They not only sing, but dance in the Spirit also! It's just incredible!" Susan laughed happily. CLANK CLANK CLANK! The sound from upstairs rang out, but once more Susan and everyone else seemed to be oblivious to the noise.

"I'd love to go with you sometime! I've never seen dancing in the spirit." I added, trying to ignore the interruptions as well. CLANK CLANIK CLANK CLANK CLANK!!! Came the angry thumping from up above. "Good grief, whatever in the world can that be?"

"Well," Susan said, drawing closer to me as she whispered "I'm afraid that's Sister Darlene up there getting a little deliverance!" She said rather excitedly.

"Oh, is that so?" I asked, concerned. Darlene had always been such a happy and cheerful girl, until recently, when she had been asking for prayer about being under the attack of Satan. She couldn't be a day over fifteen!

"Oh yes, that most certainly is so!" Susan continued to explain with relish in a hushed tone. "You see, the brethren with the gift of deliverance perceived some demonic activity in her spirit and had this scheduled, without her knowing it of course, because that would have alerted the demons to the attack against them and they could have done Lord only knows how much damage to poor Darlene!" She said, then taking a bite of the cookie from the platter on the table and extending another one for me, "You want one?" She asked, smiling.

"Uh, no, thanks anyway." I answered. Well this Darlene must not be the girl I thought she was, or she must have some serious demonic possession going on, considering the racket she was making!

"You know Dave; those demons can hold on and refuse to come out! I think that it's the cast from her broken leg that's making that banging noise on the floor." Susan said, taking another bite of the quickly disappearing cookie. The Lord gave her the faith to be healed but she allowed the devil to steel her victory by going to the doctor.

"Well, how can a person know if he is possessed or in need of this deliverance business?" I asked casually.

"Oh there's any number of behaviors, vices, even things you say or just a feeling that you give off to those around you who are sensitive in the spirit and can detect demonic possession." Susan said, now dusting off the cookie crumbs from her shawl. "Then there are other worldly activities such as smoking, drinking, swearing, even some music you listen to and some T.V. Shows you may have watched. These can all cause a possession." Susan continued.

"Well, I'd best be hitting the road. It's a long drive home, you know. Thanks for the information Susan! Bye!" I said as I quickly escaped the talk of demon possession. I was absolutely horrified by the subject and began immediately to worry if I had indeed needed some "cleaning up" as Sister Miriam had put it.

That night, I tossed and turned, rebuking Satan constantly from my mind. Finally I fell into a fitful sleep, dreaming of wolves howling, chasing me and snarling as they bit at my entire body. I grabbed their mouths with my hands, trying to pry them off of me, begging them to leave me alone. I woke up drenched in sweat, even though the temperature in my small bedroom was a bit cold.

I tiptoed to the bathroom to find the tiny bottle of aspirin, hoping to gain some relief from the dark, foreboding sense of dread in my soul. Eventually, I fell back asleep, after praying for God's protection from this evil force that I felt tightening about my throat like a vice.

The very next day, I set out for the Christian bookstore in Gulfport once more, seeking advice and knowledge on this fearful subject of demon possession. I found several pamphlets by the same preacher that Sister Parker listened to on tapes. If he was good enough for Sister Parker, he certainly is good enough for me! I bought all three of the pamphlets as well as a plain black King James Bible.

I poured over the pamphlets which told of demonic possession among Christians. The author spoke quite easily about this anomaly in horrific detail. I became absolutely convinced now that I indeed had some demonic activities in my life and I needed help!

In the past, I'd always been easily influenced by the power of suggestion. So much so that even one of the dramas on television that featured a doctor and a different case of some malady or another each week made me feel as though I were inflicted with the disease of the week. I specifically remember one night when I was around 14 years old. After watching one of these doctor episodes, I got up the courage to talk to my mother about my fears.

"Mama, do you think it might be possible that I have the same thing as that person on TV? I mean I have been feeling those very same symptoms and I think if maybe I just got checked out for it or something . . ." my voice trailed off as my mother turned to look at me in utter disbelief.

"Oh for heaven's sake, stop being such a hypochondriac!" She said setting down her mug of coffee, staring at me with a humorous grin.

"I can tell you one thing; I'm not running you kids to the doctor for every little ache and pain. Why when I was a kid, I *never* got taken to the doctor! Now I don't believe in such foolishness and I'll not hear another word on it, do you understand?" She looked at me sternly.

"But Mama, I just" I tried to answer.

"Now just relax and watch TV for awhile." She said, ending the conversation.

"I just never heard of such-a-thing in all my born days!" She said, rocking back and forth in her recline-a-rocker in the corner of the living room.

Now, I was finally learning the real causes for these problems. It was obviously the work of Satan and I most certainly would do something about it!

The next afternoon I drove over to Paul's house to discuss this whole matter with him. As I pulled in with my car, Sister Dolly was in the driveway talking to her neighbor who was also a born again Christian.

"This is Dave, a very nice Spirit-filled young man that goes to our fellowship." Sister Dolly introduced me.

"Hey" I answered shyly, although I liked the sound of her introduction. However, I wasn't totally convinced yet that I was indeed 'Spirit-filled'.

I spilled everything to Paul. It came out in a tumble of words, while Paul sat quietly, looking intently as I described in great detail my fears of demonic possession. Like Cindy and Sister Parker, he always seemed to have a little more knowledge on these matters than I did.

"Dave did you know that demons can even hide behind things that look like God? Things like pictures of Christ or statues. While you are praying to these images, the devil is stealing the worship you are trying to give to God and just waiting to leap from these things, and jump on you." Paul said.

"David, Paul, I couldn't help but overhear you talking." Sister Dolly came into the room with a kind and concerned look on her face.

"I think Sister Parker can help you. She is gifted with wisdom in such matters and could possibly give you just the right word from God or timely advice," Sister Dolly offered.

"Yeah, that's a great idea! Thanks Mom!" Paul said, kissing his mom on the cheek.

"Dave, you want to go get Cathy and then call Cindy and we can all go over to Sister Parker's together?" asked Paul. "Or we could call Cindy first before we leave."

After speaking with Cindy, it was decided that we should not include Cathy in this meeting. She just wasn't yet ready for such deep truth, so we elected to bypass picking her up and instead met Cindy at Sister Parker's house immediately.

Sister Parker's little house was a welcoming sight as we pulled up under the big oak tree with the tire swing hanging from it. "Well praise the Lord, you young'uns come on in. What brings you out my way today?" Sister Parker asked, smiling cheerfully.

"Oh Sister, you just don't know what we've been going through!" Cindy piped up as she pushed her way first into the tiny little house which today smelled of fresh pine sol. The floor shone brightly and the badly worn mop sat perched in the corner, still wet from use.

"Well honey, just sit down here and tell me all about it!" Sister Parker said sweetly.

Cindy spoke for the next thirty minutes, barely taking a breath in between tales of woe in her own life and then drawing both Paul and myself into the conversation.

Sister Parker sat listening intently to each and every word that was spoken. When finally we had exhausted everything that needed to be said, she slowly opened her tattered Bible and began to read scriptures which made us aware that we were to draw close to the Lord and purge our lives of anything that got in the way of our path to God.

"However, even with a close walk with God, there is indeed a devil and he does take up residence inside of Christians, sometimes without them even knowing it." Sister Parker said seriously.

"It's just like I thought!" Cindy said fearfully as she reached out and grabbed Paul's hand for comfort.

"Ok, now I'm convinced. This is definitely demonic and I have got to get rid of it, or them!" I said. I felt I might choke at the very thought of a demon living inside of me! I wanted only to be filled with the Holy Spirit.

"I suggest that you start the cleansing process by ridding your homes of anything and everything that could give the devil a foothold in your life!" Sister Parker warned.

"What do you mean, exactly?" I asked.

"Well, anything that doesn't glorify God, like fleshly novels, magazines, or playing cards. Even music of the world can be a cause to open up the door and call a demon into your life.

"I've got a huge collection of music and albums of all types at my house and some other things too." I said.

"Yeah, I have some games and books too." Cindy added.

"Well, I'm sure I can scrape up some things the devil is hoping to use too!" Paul said as he looked at all of us.

"Ok, let's just let the devil know we mean business! I say we have a burning at my house, out back in the old fifty-five gallon drum. We can throw everything in there and tell the devil to just get back to the pits of hell where he came from!" Sister Parker said raising her arm in victory. Amazingly, she could still show joy and victory even in times like these.

"I'm on it!" Paul said, smiling.

"Yeah, let's not waste another day. I'll go home and gather everything up and we can meet back here tonight and get this done." I said, feeling as though I couldn't stay in that house another night with those evil influences which were giving the devil a stronghold in my life.

After driving home, I went directly to my room and started to rifle threw things, throwing them in the big paper grocery sacks. I heard a soft tapping at my door.

"Who is it?" I asked.

"It's me, you goober, who do you think it is?" I heard Cathy's voice through the crack of the door. "Can I come in or what?"

"Come on in." I said hesitantly.

"What in the world are you doing? That's all your good records!" She declared.

"Be quiet before Mama hears! This is serious business that's afoot!" I spoke in a harsh whisper.

"Well clue me in, will you?" She asked, sitting down on the floor, eyes wide with excitement.

I told her everything that had been going on and our plans, but asked her not to let either Mama or Daddy know. They were just too immature in the Lord to understand the serious undertaking of spiritual warfare, and Daddy in particular would go through the roof if he knew.

"Well I want to go Dave. I have some things that need to be thrown into that fire." Cathy added solemnly.

"Oh, ok." I added slowly. I guess I didn't have a choice but to let her tag along, even though Cindy was quite serious in her warning that Cathy was clearly not ready.

We filled up sacks with all of our music, both the hard rock and the softer music. All had been tossed into the sacks. I then came upon a few albums that my brother and sister had left behind after moving out. Some of those records even had an evil look to the very cover of them. I decided after much struggling with my conscience that for their own good and the good of the household, these Satan filled albums had to be burned as well. Then I filled another sack with pictures of Jesus and small statues collected through the years of my childhood religion. It seemed like such a lifetime ago that I brought these items home from church, proud of having them in my room to look upon to remind me of Christ's suffering for our sins. I couldn't bring myself to burn them, opting for the less severe route of simply putting them into the trash that night when I brought out the garbage cans to the road which was one of my chores.

Only two lone records remained in my possession, both of them Christian music I had purchased at the mall. My brother later got wind of his disappearing albums and decided to give me a little sermon of his own, reminding me of the seventh commandment "Thou shalt not steal". I was dumbfounded that such a heathen as he would even know this scripture! After apologizing profusely, I chalked this up to persecution for the Lord. After all, I'd been told that the Bible and God's word has come as a sword between people, even family members!

Cathy and I drove in near silence to Paul's house, probably from abject fear of the event which was soon to transpire at Sister Parker's house. As my car pulled into the driveway of the little brick house where Paul lived, I could see him standing under the carport, sack in hand, filled with heaven only knows what for the burning ceremony.

"Hey, Cathy and Dave! Thanks for picking me up." Paul said setting the paper grocery sack full of records and books into the back seat of the car.

"Well I don't know about you two, but I'm scared to pieces about tonight!" Cathy said, tossing her hair as she turned to look at Paul for some sage wisdom that he usually seemed to have in great amounts at any given moment.

"Ok, then maybe I better tell you what I was going to say." Paul said biting his lower lip as though hiding a delicious secret.

"What? Go ahead and say it." I spoke up, my voice cracking in the middle of the sentence.

"I don't know now, hmmm." Paul said rolling his eyes and rubbing his chin which needed shaving.

"Oh go ahead Paul! I can take it if that's what you are worried about." Cathy said, demanding to know the undisclosed secret.

"Ok, you asked for it. You know that demons can sometimes be attached to these things and they're very angry about what we're doing. They *know* what we're planning to do to them and they don't want to relinquish control of our minds. There have been other burnings such as this where the demons have literally screamed in agony as the fire consumed them." Paul said leaning forward for emphasis.

I felt a chill go down my spine. "Paul, really? You're not putting me on, are you?" I asked.

"No Dave, this is the gospel truth man! The demons don't want to go and have been known to scream out as they are being cast into hell! Sometimes, they even jump on some bystander in the crowd." Paul said his eyes big as saucers.

"Oh dear God in heaven, I think we need to pray and plead the blood of Jesus right now!" Cathy added, her fear obvious in her shaking hands.

"Lord, we just come to you right now and plead your blood to cover us all with your protection as we do your will Lord Jesus and burn these items of idolatry. Praise you Lord, we thank you in Jesus name!" Paul prayed as we all chanted our thanks and praises in whispered tones.

"Oh look, Cindy's already there!" Paul said, seeing Cindy standing by the large rusted out fifty-five gallon drum in Sister Parker's back yard. The air was cool and crisp and there seemed to be more stars in the heavens than ever before. I could feel every leaf that crunched beneath my feet, the bags heavy in my arms. I swallowed hard and put them down beside the barrel, waiting for Sister Parker to come and begin the ceremony.

"Praise the Lord, y'all all made it here fine! I was worried. Sometimes the devil tries to interfere and harm God's children when they take steps to send them back on their way!" Sister Parker said looking around our little circle, making eye contact with each one of us. "Now, let's join hands and pray."

As we prayed and sang choruses, my heart still beat rapidly, not knowing what would happen when the wretched worldly objects were destroyed. Then Sister Parker motioned for me to begin. I picked up the entire bag and tossed it into the fire. Sparks flew up into the trees, catching and burning the dried leaves on the branch which hung down. It seemed as though the fire's hot tongue of flames licked at the tree, trying to destroy it along with the bits and pieces of our former lives that now were melting into one heap.

"Well praise the Lord, it's done!" Sister Parker said. "Now, I have something else to tell you. "Under submission to my shepherd, brother

Wendall, it was my duty to inform him of tonight's service as unto the Lord." Sister Parker glanced down in humility. "In his wisdom, he has said that he already sensed a problem and decided that next Tuesday night instead of the regular classes, a special deliverance service is to be held. Anyone who feels they've been under the attack of the devil or in need of deliverance will be asked to come to the front. The brethren who are gifted with the spirit of discernment will be casting out the demons." Sister Parker looked again at each of us.

I could feel a knot forming in my throat and no amount of swallowing would push it down as my heart beat so rapidly that I thought that Paul, Cathy or Cindy might hear it.

"I'm to counsel all of you to begin a holy fast on Monday going through Tuesday. This is a way to starve out the demons as well as to teach you to say 'no' to the fleshly things of this world." Sister Parker concluded. "Now I will be in prayer for each one of you to have special protection until that time. The demons know what we are planning and will try anything to prevent it from happening. See to it that you use extra caution in all that you do from here on out."

"Oh thank you Jesus, hallelujah!" Cindy shouted with one arm in the air and tears streaming down her face. "Paul, will you and David come and get me Tuesday? I won't feel safe driving alone." Cindy said touching Paul's arm.

"Sure Cindy, that's no problem." I answered quietly, hoping no one noticed that I had been fidgeting nearly uncontrollably. How could I wait until Tuesday night services? The ever-present fear of Satan taking over my mind loomed over me like a huge, dark storm cloud. Jesus had admonished His disciples not to be anxious for anything, so if I'm anxious, it's obviously caused by Satan!

As Monday rolled around, I nervously and seriously entered into my time of fasting and prayer. I decided to call Paul Monday evening to see how he was holding up to the deprivation.

"Hey man, how's the fast going?" I asked casually on the phone.

"Well it was tough going today. I was under the attack by Satan to eat some French fries in the school cafeteria. Why did they just have to make today burger and fries day? I think the devil had a hand in that! But anyway, I'm doing better now since I came home and Mom fixed me a milk shake.

"A milk shake? I thought we had to fast?" I asked astonished.

"That's fasting! If you can drink it, it doesn't count as food, David. Didn't you know that?" Paul said with a chuckle as though I must be quite the immature Christian.

"Well, actually, no, I didn't know that. But now that I do, I think I will run to McDonalds and get me one too!" I said, feeling as though someone had just told me it was Christmas and I didn't realize it until the day was very nearly over. "Who told you about this?" I asked curious about who had clued him in.

"Cindy happened to mention it to me today when she was having a Barq's root beer." Paul said taking another long suck from the milk shake straw.

"From now on, feel free to let me know any of these 'truths', Paul!" I said joking.

"Right on brother. I hear ya!" Paul chuckled.

As I drove to McDonald's, I went extra slow, trying to avoid any accidents that the devil might have planned for me tonight. Having been taught by the brethren that the Bible also instructed us that God's people were to obey all laws of the land, I wouldn't dare go one mile per hour over the posted speed limit. I could hear my stomach growling like a bear just coming out of hibernation!

That had to be the best milk shake I ever had in my life. How did Jesus do it? How in the world did He fast for so long in that desert and I could barely make it a day? I still had another whole day to go. "Lord help me" I heard myself say out loud.

I slept fitfully that night as wolves chased me once more into deep pits where I couldn't escape their snarls and sharp teeth. Some of them had stared at me with glowing red eyes. Only one more day, I thought as I struggled to fast hour by hour.

On our ride to the House of Praise, all of us were both excited about the coming meeting, as well as fearful.

"Mmm, look at that over there Paul!" Cindy said pointing to a billboard with some ham and eggs that looked smoking hot and delicious. "Have you ever been there?" She said smiling.

"No, but it looks mighty good to me about now!" Paul said laughing and holding his growling stomach.

"Oh wait, look, that one's even better!" I said pointing to yet another billboard with a juicy, sizzling hot steak, and a giant baked potato slathered in butter and sprinkled with bacon. The billboards continued to loom ahead of us.

"I have never noticed so many food signs before! Did they just put them up today or something?" Cathy said.

"No silly, we are all just starving!" Paul said playfully slapping Cathy's head.

"Don't make me go back there and rebuke you Paul, cuz you know I can do it!" Cathy teased.

"Oh yeah, you and who else, little girl?" Paul said popping her on top of her head once more.

"Ok, now Sister Cathy, this is not becoming to the Lord! Your behavior should be chaste and humble. But then, you'll learn that as you grow into greater maturity." Cindy said with an air of superiority.

"Yeah, little girl!" Paul said leaning over and pinching her arm.

"Ok, I'm fixing to come back there and fix you good Paul! . . . . I'll learn to be chaste and humble tomorrow!" Cathy said turning around and popping Paul square on the head. "Ha! Told ya so!"

"Alright, I give." Paul said rubbing his head.

"She packs a wallup Dave!" Paul said whistling.

"I know she does! She's hit me enough times!" I said laughing nervously, while my head was actually about to split in two from the headache I was experiencing on this fearful night.

"I think we should all be getting ourselves into the proper spirit for tonight. After all, we are still in a state of fasting and prayer." Cindy rebuked.

We arrived at the fellowship and singing could already be heard coming from inside of the old house. "Clap your hands, all ye people, shout unto God with a voice of triumph. Clap your hands, all ye people, shout unto God with a voice of praise!" The evening had begun in earnest as we each settled into our places and yet another "victory over the devil" chorus began: "In the name of Jesus. In the name of Jesus, demons will have to flee. In the name of Jesus, in the name of Jesus, we have the victory!"

At the end of the chorus, one of the elders, stood to his feet and with much authority declared: "Satan, we rebuke you in the name of Jesus and you are commanded in His holy name to leave this building right now! Flee, flee you coward, and get back to the pit of hell! We command you in the authority given us by our Lord!" Shouts of praise erupted throughout the crowd as people stood to their feet in praise and worship, joining and commanding Satan to leave the house of the Lord immediately. High praises burst forth and seemed to shake the very gates of hell! Surely the devil was defeated and in retreat tonight!

"Brothers and Sisters in Christ, "Brother Wendell's' voice boomed out. "Come forth all who are in need of deliverance from the bondages of Satan." He raised one fist up to heaven and shook it. "Come, come and demand your freedom. It's right here, but you have to come and take it!" The sound of his voice caused many to start flowing to the front of the room. Some came with hands over their faces, others with hands lifted in praise, tears streaming down their faces as they voiced their love for God.

My heart pounded as I felt the eyes of every person in the room surely had to be upon me. I could nearly feel the clawing of demons inside my belly as they struggled to keep their hold on me and drive me out of my mind.

Cathy came and kneeled on one side of me. Then Cindy and Paul knelt slowly and reverently on my other side. The sound of people coughing and gagging could be heard from behind me. The deliverance had now begun!

I felt an urge to cough a small amount as the feeling of a strong hand was placed on my shoulder. The elders surrounded us from behind and went from person to person to pray for God's holy release within each soul. The sound of his sincere prayer filled my entire being with a sense of warmth and love. I felt tears streaming down my face as my own personal release exploded from deep within me. I was free! I was filled from my head to my toes, with the Spirit of God almighty!

"I'm so glad, that Jesus set me free, yes I'm so glad that Jesus set me free!" Someone started to sing as the entire crowd joined in the happy song of freedom and joy.

"Praise God, Dave and you too, Paul!" Cindy came up and wrapped her arms around both of us. Her eyes were glistening from tears. She too was experiencing the all-encompassing feeling of God's peace and freedom. I looked and saw Cathy with her arms raised and singing the soprano harmony to the song of victory. This was truly a night to remember.

"Brothers, Sisters, there is an admonition from the Lord that you all must hear." Brother Wendall took the podium once again, his shirt sleeves rolled up to his elbows and his hair, usually pulled back, now lay in streaks across his forehead, evidence of the hard work he had done in delivering the people from their demons. "It is written that the demons could return and bring seven times the number of what they once were if allowed. This is serious business, my people. Let's go forth and live our lives in such a way as to forbid these demons from re-entering their homes."

That word from brother Wendall had the effect of planting a small mustard seed of doubt within my heart. But I quickly brushed the feeling aside as our joyful car ride back began with everyone stopping at McDonalds for something to eat!

"What are you going to have Sister Cindy, praise the Lord!?" Paul asked Cindy laughing out loud.

"Well bless God; I think I'll have the double cheeseburger; fries and a large shake brother Paul!" Cindy said so loudly that everyone in the place turned to look.

"How about you, Brother Dave and Sister Cathy?" Paul continued on his spree.

"I think I'll have the halleluiah hamburger with no pickles and a coke brother Paul!" Cathy answered, barely able to contain her laughter.

"Well amen Sister Cathy, I do believe I'll have the same!" I chimed in with the fun.

"Well praise the Lord everyone!" The lady with the cokes, taking our order said as she slapped her hand on the counter before marching off singing "Onward Christian Soldiers, as off key as I'd ever heard in my life."

Several customers and employees burst out laughing and even clapping as we all took our trays to eat our first real meal in two days.

That night as I lay in my bed in the bedroom on Linda Lane, the gentle cool breeze blew in through the sheer white panel curtains. I covered myself with delight at the feeling. Slipping my arms from beneath the cotton covers, I raised my arms toward the heavens, thanking God for this sweet release. I could picture Jesus walking beside me on the sandy beaches as I drifted off to a deep and peaceful sleep. The days ahead were permeated with thoughts of a bright and happy future walking with the Lord!

CHAPTER 4

FROM THE MOUNTAIN TO
THE VALLEY

I'm on the top of the world
Looking down on creation
And the only explanation I can find
Is the love that I've found
Ever since you've been around—
Your love put me at the top of the world
(Carpenters)

The Thanksgiving holiday found me comfortably snuggled in bed, enjoying the luxury of resting past the break of day due to the A & P being closed up tight for the holiday. Drifting in and out of dream sleep, I slowly rolled over to doze off once more, enjoying the cool breeze floating through my slightly raised window. I could smell the faint scent of wood smoke from a nearby fireplace. The rich, earthy notes blended with the sound of fluttering dry autumn leaves to make a wonderful symphony, lulling me gently into a deeper realm of comfortable relaxation, falling peacefully into the delicious state of sleep.

"Time to get up young'un's! Don't let the sun rise and set on your back sides!" The voice of my mother rang out from the nearby kitchen, jangling my nerves with the clattering of pots and pans as she scurried about preparing our noontime meal of roasted chicken, cornbread dressing, gravy, rolls, baked beans and sweet potato pie. We rarely ever feasted on turkey for the holidays. I always preferred chicken to the dry, stringy meat of the turkey anyway.

"So much for sleeping in." I grumbled to myself as I was forced to awaken and make my bed before dressing and going into the living room where I could hopefully watch something on television while the cooking of the feast commenced.

As I combed my hair, I noticed a light heartedness about my countenance that came from deep within my spirit. Smiling into the mirror, I could see a twinkle of happiness reflecting in my eyes. I *was* happy! I had the wonderful, overwhelming sense of peace and gratitude to God.

"Thank you Lord Jesus. Praise you Lord." I said as I raised my hands freely in worship to my creator, my God and the rock of my salvation. I allowed the Holy Spirit to pray through me, as I adored my heavenly Father. Gone were the old, dry traditional prayers I had committed to memory so many years ago. I had been taught a prayer for nearly every given situation in life and spent hours in memorization of them throughout my early childhood. Now, my prayers were simple and much shorter. A thought from deep within tried to surface and alert me to the fact that my current prayers were also quite one dimensional at times. I must push that thought back. I'd been moving forward for God and nothing would be allowed to draw me back into those traditions.

"MMmmm, that smells good!" I said as the scent of hot coffee aroused my senses. I made my way to the pot on the stove and poured myself a steaming cup of the fresh, black brew. I took a sip and turned my head toward the living room when I heard the clear, high voice of my sister, Cathy singing a catchy new tune.

"I'm on the top of the world looking down on creation and the only explanation I can find, is the love that I've found ever since you've been around. Your love's put me on the top of the world." She sang with gusto and enthusiasm, as she always did.

"Good morning brother. How do you like the song the Lord just gave me?" She asked grinning with a twinkle in her eye.

"I really do like that." I said, without even the slightest smile, as my eyes narrowed considering this "gift" the Lord had given to, of all people, *her*! She was but a mere novice in her walk with the Lord compared to someone as spiritually mature as myself!

This must be some sort of tragic oversight on God's part! Perhaps I needed to make myself known more clearly in my fervent prayers to the Lord, enlightening him as to my goals and wishes! Yes, that *had* to be it! All I needed to do was *ask*! The Lord was surely just trying to show me by this situation how much more he would bless me if only I would *ask* him! I had just *assumed* the Lord must surely know that the most momentous goal in my entire life at this point in time, was to receive some sort of marvelous revelation directly from the throne of God! He seemed to be revealing things to most everyone among my friends as well as the brethren at the Farm. Perhaps, I'd be next in line!

Cathy began to laugh, as she looked me dead in the face. To my surprise, I was the brunt of some sort of joke that only she was in on.

"Oh Dave, you silly thing! It's the latest hit by the Carpenter's! Gee whiz, why don't you listen to the radio a little more like you used to and maybe you would know!" Cathy nearly cackled as she held her stomach and laid across the sofa, peels of laughter ringing out at what I considered to be a most ill-humored attack against me. I could feel a righteous indignation rising from deep within. It was time to put my fresh little sister in her place and rebuke her in the Lord!

"Cathy I don't know why you think this is funny! I'll have you know that I'm honoring the Lord, as well *you* should be, by *not* listening to the radio anymore! It's full of nothing but worldly music of the devil as any *mature* Christian would know!" I felt immediate relief when I saw the look of shame that came over her face at this little eye-opening word from the Lord. It also didn't hurt any to know that in fact she had *not* received any sort of gift from the Lord! I felt utterly vindicated and rightly so!

"Cathy, get in here! I'll need some help in the kitchen today with all of this extra cookin'." Mama's voice rang out.

"Hmph!" I said nodding toward Cathy. I had the final laugh in this little situation. The Lord was seeing to it that she was rebuked all the way around!

"David, go help your Daddy get the extra leaf put into the table. Now you kids get a move on!" Mama's added order stung my pride a bit as Cathy turned and smirked at me as we both headed toward the kitchen in line like a row of ducks.

It was noon on the dot and the Thanksgiving feast was laid out on the little kitchen table. I could hardly wait to dig in! My mother ran a tight ship and she never failed to have the meals ready at precisely noon. Daddy had gotten used to the schedule and fell right into the routine sitting at the head of the table.

We all sat in silence as he began the blessing prayer. "Bless us oh Lord and these Thy gifts, which we are about to receive . . ."

"Oh thank you Jesus, we just praise you Jesus." I looked over at my sister, who I thought had clearly taken leave of her senses as she offered up praises with her arms raised, as though she were at the fellowship! However, refusing to be outdone, I decided quickly that it would be best if I showed appropriate praise as well. It was high time that my poor lost Father was witnessed to anyway! For that matter, I figured my mother's spiritual life was in need of a little shaking up as well since she had never yet come out to the House of Praise either, although she had promised us she would check it out someday!

"Well, I didn't know if this was a Thanksgiving meal or some sort of big tent revival! What in the world is going on around here anyway?" My father's voiced boomed after he finished the prayer. He was beside himself with curiosity now, and a little on edge that he'd been left out of something of observable importance to us.

"I was just praising my wonderful Lord and Savior. He is worthy to be praised you know." My sister's voice quickly answered, equally strong in her demeanor as she faced off with our father.

My mother's eyes pleaded with my sister, her meaning clear. The unspoken words hung in the room. "Please don't do or say anything to ruin Thanksgiving Day after I've worked so hard preparing this meal!"

"Well?" My Dad now turned and looked to me for an answer. Mama glanced at me with just a little hope in her eyes now, as the clock on the wall seemed to tick loudly enough to wake the dead. My tongue felt thick and heavy, and the words in my mind muddled together as my heart pounded in my brain. I could only think to say the words 'what she said', but knowing this not to be the proper response; I held my peace and tried to think of something more appropriate as quickly as possible. All eyes bored holes into me at the same time. Suddenly, an idea formed in my mind.

"Well maybe if you listen to some cassette tapes I recorded out at the fellowship, you'd get a better idea of what's going on. I can play them for you after we eat if you like. I think it'll clarify most everything." I offered quietly.

Glancing at my mother I could see the tension around her eyes and mouth as she winced, awaiting Daddy's reply. She peeked back over at my sister, with a pitiful look, but Cathy, ever the radical, stared straight ahead unapologetically, further irritating Mama's fragile nerves. Cathy clearly was not playing the game. "Well, I was wondering when this family was going to include me in on everything that's been going on around here in secret!" Daddy said, his jaw clenching and unclenching in clear aggravation. "I'll listen to those tapes, and I hope it explains a few things! But for now, let's finish our meal, and hopefully without the Hallelujah's or Amen's! Honestly, I thought Oral Roberts was going to walk in here for a minute there! For crying' out loud kids! Sheesh!" He said with utter disgust. Then he immediately switched gears as he turned to my mother and said, "Mama, this looks like a wonderful feast you've prepared."

"Thank you Daddy." Mama said looking at him with great relief on her face. Clearly she was off the hook in his sight and was not blamed for this outburst.

Well, we had certainly dodged a bullet this time! Still I wondered who in the world Oral Roberts was. He must be some old fogey from my Dad's time, along with the phrase "tent-revival" which up until this very day, I'd never heard in my life.

As soon as the delicious meal was eaten, Cathy and Mama proceeded to clear the table, putting things away and washing up the kitchen dishes. I went to my bedroom and dug out the now familiar tapes of the high praises. Cathy came in and immediately sat on my bed, raising her arms and singing in beautiful worshipful notes of praise.

Daddy soon walked in and sat down on the corner of my bed looking on in amazement at the sounds coming from the little tape recorder. By the time the first high praises had finished, I quickly forwarded the tape to the second praises that had been sung. My Dad's face was solemn and I thought I saw a tear in his eye as he listened intently to the beautiful music.

"Mama, come in here! Dave, play that one more time." Daddy called out as Mama quickly scurried into the bedroom.

"Yeah Gene, what is it?" Mama said holding the wet dishcloth in one hand.

"That's the most beautiful music I've ever heard in my life!" Daddy said sincerely as he looked at Mama.

"Yeah." Mama echoed with a puzzled look on her face. "Do they always sing like that where you kids have been running off to? What's it called anyway, a glory house?" Daddy asked.

"Yes, they sing high praises every time they have worship services, and it's not a glory house. It's 'the House of Praise!'" Sometimes we just call it the fellowship, Cathy answered quickly.

"Dave, have you been back to St. Thomas lately?" Daddy asked turning to me while I fumbled with the cassette tape.

"Not since September." I answered fingering my hair out of my face and shoving my hands in my pockets.

"Uh huh. Well, I can't say I'm surprised. I knew something was up around here. Maybe I'll just go out to that fellowship place myself sometime." Daddy said in a way that seemed as though he were almost asking permission.

"Uh, yeah, that would be great. I think you'd like the brethren out there. It's different." I added in a state of shock. Wow, the Lord really *had* been moving and blessing us this day! I'll have to get in the kitchen to use the phone and call Paul and Cindy when everyone has cleared out and I can have a little privacy to tell them all about the news of the day! Cathy stared at me with a grin on her face after our parents had left the room.

"Praise the Lord!" Cathy said in a quiet, excited whisper! "What a surprise, huh?"

"No kidding! The Lord really is working through us! I have an idea, Cathy, about another way the Lord might use us." I said as I slowly closed the door.

"Well, tell me!" Cathy's hazel eyes grew large with anticipation.

"Well, you know how Mama and Aunt Clarice haven't spoken since that last spat way awhile back?" I asked.

"Yeah, I don't know what in the world happened between them in the kitchen that day, but it ended up with Mama crying and Aunt Clarice swearing she'd never 'never darken our door again!'" Cathy said remembering the day of the argument.

"Well I have an idea that maybe we should just drop in on her and tell her about the Lord and our experience out at the House of Praise." I explained.

"Ooooh, great idea! When do we go?" Cathy was just about ready to snatch her purse and jump in the car.

"Well hang on! We can't go today, but let's pray about going out there Saturday." I offered.

"Let's pray right now!" Cathy added as she took my hand and led the prayer.

"Lord we just come before you in Jesus name, and we just thank you Lord Jesus for all that you've done for us and in our lives, Jesus. Now we ask that you guide us and be with us as we go to share your word with our Aunt Clarice. Help us to show her your way, Lord and open her heart to receive your word in Jesus name!" Cathy prayed almost a little too loudly.

"Thank you Jesus, Amen, Lord. Thank you, Jesus!" I said with my eyes closed as my free hand rose in worship. Cathy and I prayed together a lot here lately. It was comforting to know that we were serving the Lord together and could count on each other for support in everything that we did. I could share my thoughts with her and she would pray with me at any time.

Aunt Clarice had always been one of my favorite aunts. Being my mother's sister, she was as southern as fried chicken and grits. She was the happier of the two sisters and nearly always wore a smile. Her husband, Clem, worked with Daddy at the Post Office. Both of them were letter carriers and their friendship also lasted into the weekends by frequently fishing together. Many times, they planned their all night flounder-gigging trips with great anticipation of bringing home a huge mess of the large, flat, oblong fish for their families. My mother would set up the old beat up metal table out back, ready with fish-scalers, knives and containers to freeze the fish filets into small allotments for family meals.

Aunt Clarice and Uncle Clem lived in a nicer section of Long Beach, in a modest three-bedroom brick home. Their children, Pam and Terry were just about the age of Cathy and I. Their youngest, Amy, would join in and play with us on the special occasions when we would visit their home. With every visit, Aunt Clarice would offer each of us a Coca-Cola and treats like ice cream and chips and would allow us to enjoy them in the other room with our cousins, while the 'grownups' talked in the kitchen.

She had a way about her that was both delightful and irritating all at the same time. This due in large part to the fact that she had a more inquisitive nature than a cat! Indeed, I believe she would have made a quite successful newspaper reporter, had she chosen that line of work.

That Sunday afternoon, Cathy and I found ourselves parked in Aunt Clarice's driveway, ready to minister to her needs and solve this family rift with the love of God our Father. We joined hands and said a short prayer before walking what felt like a mile before reaching the little white front door. This was a now a place that somehow felt alien and not at all like the friendly retreat which I had so enjoyed to visit.

I knocked quietly and in no time at all, there she was, just as stunned as a deer in the headlights, standing before us with her mouth gaping open.

"Uh hum" I cleared my throat awkwardly. "Aunt Clarice, I just came over to tell you that Jesus loves you and so do I." I said sheepishly. I could feel the heat rising from my neck to my face, knowing that I most certainly had to be just about the shade of a ripe radish at this point.

"Yeah, me too." Cathy echoed.

Within an instant, she drew us both to her and began to laugh, kissing us both soundly on the cheek and standing aside for us to come into her home.

"Y'all want a coke?" She asked before turning to Pam. "Pam, grab them a Coke out of the fridge honey, will you please for your Mama?" Pam smiled sweetly as she withdrew the bottle opener and popped the steel crimped tops off of two Coca-Cola's. The lovely white smoke flowed from each bottle as she graciously handed them to us.

It began to seem as though there had never been any time in which we had not been on speaking terms with our Aunt and cousins. All was as it had always been, except our message. We told her of our newfound "body" of believers in D'Iberville and described in detail the high praises and inspired messages directly from the Lord, which surely she had never heard before. After all, where else *was* there to go to receive such a bounty of blessings? The House of Praise was *the* place to go for anyone who was truly seeking God's word!

By the time we arrived back home, the sound of Mama's voice could be heard on the front porch as she stood by the screened kitchen door chatting away with her sister who had arrived there before us. Sometimes I wondered if Aunt Clarice had one of those transporters such as I'd seen on Star Trek. As we walked up the drive from my car, the two sisters continued to talk and laugh as though the rift had never happened! Cathy nudged me in the arm and we both grinned at one another. The Lord was truly working through us this weekend! Praise His Name!

Sunday afternoon found us scurrying quickly around the house and getting ready for the night's believer's gathering. "Cathy you better hurry and get ready to leave. Services will be starting at the fellowship and I don't want to be late." I advised my sister, who was in the annoying habit of doing much primping before going anywhere.

"Oh, yeah, that's right! Let me go!" Cathy said excitedly as she whisked herself back into the tiny corner bedroom, closing the door behind her.

As soon as I entered the now familiar doors of the House of Praise, that wonderful feeling of being "home" washed over me. I could feel the joy welling up inside my soul in anticipation of the stirringly emotional high praises which transported me to a heavenly realm of peace and happiness.

"Oh Brother Dave, come over here. I have some news for you!" Brother Wendall said; grabbing my arm and pulling me to a private corner of the room.

"Oh, what is it?" I asked wondering what on earth this news could be. "Well, there's an opening at the store where I work at the mall and I already spoke to the manager about you. He wants to see you for an interview!" Brother Wendall smiled from ear to ear. "You get this job and you would be off every Sunday and free to come to worship! You wouldn't have to worry about ever being called in to work on a Sunday again since the store is closed on Sunday's. Oh and you will never have to work past 6:00 on weeknights, because the mall shuts down at 6:00. Well of course right before Christmas they are opened until 9:00, but that's just for a couple of weeks. Are you interested?"

"Sure! That would be great! I'd be free to come to more of the services y'all have out here. I really appreciate it Brother Wendall!" I said sincerely. "What an answer to prayer!" I added.

"Yes Dave, the Lord had showed unto me the desires of your heart and I was moved to speak for you when this opportunity arose. All things in God's own good timing, Brother Dave!" Brother Wendall said slapping me on the back and leading me toward the rest of the brethren gathered in the main room.

The praises that night were spectacular! God moved through many folks with special words of prophecy for the flock, which flowed directly from the throne of God Almighty! The wonderful feeling of euphoria flowed through me as I praised the Lord with all my heart, knowing that He was allowing me the special privilege of spending more time here, in God's own house, learning His word and praising Him through this new job opportunity.

The day of my interview was arranged the following morning and the time for the interview came and went with great speed. Before I knew it, I had landed a new job and was preparing to give notice to the old A & P grocery store. A bit of sadness crept into my mind as I remembered the fun times spent there, joking and playing around with my old friends Daphne, Maurice and all the gang. Funny, though, they no longer played the same role in my life. God had weaned me from my former ways and even these friends. I forged past any doubts and gave a one-week notice. I was ready to begin my new life and my new job.

"Hey Dave, sorry to hear you're leaving us, man." Daphne said during our lunch break.

"Thanks, but I guess it's time." I added quietly.

"You're still going out to that House of Praise place, aren't you?" Daphne asked quietly. I could sense a feeling of genuine concern from her.

"Yeah, it's been great Daphne. You ought to come out there sometime. You just would be blown away by how the Lord is working out there! I mean it's like nothing you could have ever seen before, I promise you that!" I added excitedly. It would be great to have Daphne join the brethren and become part of our spiritual family.

"Thanks, but I'm happy where I am." She added taking a swig of her Coke. "Listen, you be careful out there, ok, Dave?" Daphne said, her light green eyes penetrating as she seemed to look deep within me, in a searching way.

"I don't know what you mean by 'careful', but I can tell you that the word of the Lord is right on out there, like nowhere else." I said a bit taken aback that she would think I would feel the need to exercise caution of any sort!

"Well I've heard rumors here and there about that place, I mean about some funny business going on, maybe even with drugs and some other things, worse than drugs. Some people are calling it the "funny farm." Daphne added trying to warn me.

"Well I can tell you right now, there is nothing but worship and praise going on out there. Maybe those people just don't understand how we are *supposed* to be worshipping God and the devil is speaking through them to keep people from finding the real way!" I added, feeling the sting of persecution which all of God's faithful must endure, just as the disciples had.

"Ok Dave. I'll let it go. We'll sure miss you around here. It won't be the same." Daphne added kindly.

"Yeah, well, I'll drop by and see y'all from time to time." I added, somehow knowing that I never would. I'd found the true meaning of life and now I only desired to immerse myself in the experience and be with others who felt the same as I did; others who were seeking the truth and finding it right there at the Farm!

Still though, Daphne's words haunted me. My own brother, Ronnie, had given me a similar warning not many days ago. He even seemed a little frustrated that I wouldn't listen to him. Well, what could he possibly know about it, I assured myself. After all, he hasn't even been spiritually born again.

My new route to work seemed unusually long while I listened to the easy listening station, which was certainly more edifying music than the mighty 690,. I tried to convince myself that the new radio station of choice was better than my old favorite. I took advantage of the drawn-out nine-mile drive by looking at the splendid view of the ocean. The waves sparkled like diamonds against the robin's egg blue sky. The familiar sights of the shrimp boats and gulls hawking as they swooped around the nets rigged high in the sky and the people walking hand in hand on the sandy shores, served to calm my nerves, which seemed to be jangled these days whenever I was not at the fellowship.

"Now where did I put those tracts?" I mumbled to myself after parking the car near the entrance of the store. "Oh there they are. Thank you Lord!" Surely He had shown me where the hidden tracts were so that I might witness to all the lost souls who would be shopping that day. One of my new duties at work was to box up Christmas purchases in the signature packages of the store. I would quietly slip a Christian tract under the intended gift for the customer's loved ones and quickly enfold it in tissue paper, closing the carton neatly, to be opened Christmas morning.

I smiled to myself as I envisioned the surprise on the people's faces when after seeing their Christmas sweater; a gospel tract would fall out, inviting them to come to know the Lord. So many lost souls! All of them floundering about in this world, going to church where they only *thought* they were hearing God's word. Oh if only they knew the error of their ways! If only they could taste what the House of Praise had to offer, the life, the love, the fellowship and worship! Surely there is no other place on this planet that could measure up. God had absolutely set upon this fellowship the task of being the door to *truly* knowing God's love and being born again. Everything else is just folly!

Considering the fact that the owners of the store where I now am employed are Jewish, I felt it best to keep my evangelization tactics and ministry to myself. They probably are not ready to see the light just yet. Someday maybe the opportunity to witness to them would come about and they, too, could see the light! That would truly be a great witness for the Lord!

When my usual mid-week day off rolled around, I felt a burst of happiness when I awoke, remembering that today, Larry and Dean from the fellowship were going to come and visit me. They lived at the local Air Force base in Biloxi and were two of my favorite friends.

The aging 1960's VW van pulled into my driveway with a distinct rattle and squeak. I smiled to myself as I put my Bible down and walked out onto the front porch, the screen door smacking loudly behind me.

"Hey Brother Dave! Praise the Lord! So good to see you and have some fellowship with you today!" Dean said, reaching out his hand to shake mine. Larry reached around and patted my shoulder firmly.

"Yeah, come on in. Y'all want some coffee?" I asked trying to be sociable.

"Oh, you southerners and your coffee." Dean smiled, teasing me. "No, I don't drink coffee."

"Oh ok. Well, I told Paul that you were coming over today and he wants us to go over and pick him up while we bum around town." I added.

I pulled my car into the Green Acres subdivision dotted with little brick ranch homes. "Look at Paul, y'all." I said laughing. Paul was standing in his driveway with his Bible in hand, waving and jumping up and down to get our attention.

"Get in you fool!" Dean said, joking and laughing.

"Well Brother Dean, you could burn in hell for saying that! No man is to say to another that he is a fool." Paul said, joking back with him and quoting the scripture.

As we drove across the railroad tracks and took a turn to the right where the little road looked green, shady, and nice for a drive, the small sign "You are entering Pass Christian" popped out from under the leaves of a deep green magnolia tree.

"Hey, I know where we are! The Tanner's live just ahead on the left, facing the ocean, in that old southern restored home." Larry added smiling, as though remembering something fondly, but with a bit of sadness.

"Oh wow, that's really beautiful! Looks like a mini Gone With The Wind, huh?" Paul added.

"Sure does! How do you know them, Larry?" I asked.

"Well, a few months back, I heard about a prayer meeting that was held in the Tanner's house. I was told they believed in the gifts of the spirit and that all faiths were equally welcome to come and join. Me and another airman went and had such a great time. Brother Wendall came along with us, too. Dr. Tanner is a down to earth teacher of the Word. Then, after the prayer meeting is over, Mrs. Tanner has the entire table filled with great things to eat, everything from scones and cookies, to baked ham, spiced tea, home made breads, you name it. We all stayed around and fellowshipped and had a great time." Larry said rather wistfully.

"Well why did you quit going?" Dean asked.

"Oh, well, Brother Wendall has forbidden it." Gary said as a sad look crossed his face for a moment.

"Why do you think he did that?" Paul asked quietly.

"He said something about them being rabble-rousers. But I have to say Dr. and Mrs. Tanner were two of the kindest, best people I ever met in my entire life," Larry said, turning his head back to see the Tanner's home disappearing from view.

"It's not always easy to be submissive to the will of the Lord, but He has given our shepherds the wisdom to guide and teach us all things holy and righteous. I think it shows your spiritual growth that you have honored God's will by your submission to Brother Wendall. He has so much wisdom!" Paul added, his face and eyes solemn.

I thought to myself about Brother Wendall; his fiery preaching; his winning personality and his top of the line salesmanship at work. No one could outsell him! He was the store's biggest and best producer and was honored each week during our sales meetings. It must be the Lord blessing his sales because he is so faithful to Him. I wish the Lord would bless and help me with my sales. I was dead last and seemed never to be able to have the right things to say to the shoppers when asked a question. My shy nature would take over, as I would answer each question asked as honestly as I could. It usually ended with the customer leaving empty handed, and me without a sale.

"Hey Brother Dave, look at that gas needle. It's on dead empty, man!" Dean said. "In Jesus name . . . . fill it up!" He added, half jokingly.

I caught myself looking at the needle, hoping in the back of my mind to see it actually move. It did finally move, but not before I stuck the nozzle in the tank at the new self-service isle at Smitty's Service station.

"Hey do you remember the hymn called Precious Lord?" Dean asked.

"Well, I think I do, but I'm not positive." Larry answered.

"Precious Lord, take my hand. Lead me on. Let me stand." Dean's voice sang quietly and with much emotion through the entire first verse. I'd never heard such a beautiful hymn.

"I miss singing that hymn." Dean said quietly.

"But still, isn't it great that we all now go to a place where only the *full* gospel is preached?" I added.

"Praise the Lord brother Dave, you speak the truth!" Paul added.

"Yeah, it really is. There just is no other place out there like the House of Praise!" Larry said smiling.

"Amen!" Dean added with a bright smile.

The rest of the afternoon seemed to fly by in my little car on that clear December day, which was coming to a close all too soon. I had been so lonely all my life, especially in my high school years. I was so glad to finally have friends to chum around with on an otherwise boring day off. Days away from the fellowship now seemed to be somewhat of a struggle. My entire social circle was the body of believers at the House of Praise. My happiness and joy revolved around the times spent there. I counted the days in between when the next service was to be held. So this day off was a special day, a day of wonderful, uplifting fellowship with true believers.

As Larry and Dean pulled out of my driveway, the van rattling and squeaking; we all waved happily. I hoped they'd come more often and spend some time with me. That was, however, the last time their old van would ever drive down Linda Lane again.

As Christmas drew ever closer, my sales at the department store in the mall didn't show much improvement. However, Brother Wendall continued to break records, joking with both employees and customers alike, charming everyone with whom he came into contact.

My headaches and ensuing panic attacks grew increasingly worse and I found myself continually traveling toward the back stock room in order to rebuke Satan and plead the blood of Jesus for protection from demons. On one such occasion, after performing what had become my usual routine; I stood at the entrance of the stock room, catching my breath and willing my heart to stop pounding. I overheard the distinct voice of Brother Wendall talking with one of the other employees.

"Yes, yes, and did you see the way he *walks*?" Brother Wendall said, followed by low chuckling. "He looks like he's about to fly right out of here!"

"Oh Wendall, you are too much!" The voice of the warehouse manager said in low tones. "You know how to make a dull day go by quicker, man! You stay out of that girly guy's way in the bathroom now, ya hear?" The manager walked away with both men in fits of laughter.

I'd never heard brother Wendall joke in such a vulgar fashion before. Surely the warehouse manager had initiated this and brother Wendall was just going along with him.

This would not be the last time I would stumble upon a conversation not meant for my ears in which I would distinctly hear Brother Wendall involved in a course joke or making rude and disparaging comments about others. I fought hard to push all such negative thoughts to the back of my mind; knowing this must be nothing more than the devil, trying to twist things around and cause doubt to enter into my spirit. Brother Wendall's wisdom was known far and wide. He was reputed to be a most chaste man, promoting only high morals among the brethren. Any doubts in my mind were obviously the work of Satan! Perhaps another visit to Sister Parker would be in order. I feared that the demons once cast out had now come back with seven times the number! I determined I would talk to Brother Wendall about the possibility of another exorcism and get his wisdom on the matter.

"Brother Dave! Let's take a coffee break together, shall we?" Brother Wendall said slapping me congenially on the back.

"Sure I'd like that. I've wanted to talk to you about some things." I said, pulling my wallet from my back pocket to buy a Coke.

"Well that's a coincidence, because I have some big news to tell you, but you have to keep it to yourself. You know not everyone is as mature as you are with the Lord and they just aren't ready for the level of truth that you are walking in." Brother Wendall said confidentially.

"There are going to be some changes at the fellowship. It's time we brought things into order. You know the Jesus movement is dead from lack of discipline. The entire flock across this country is in chaos from *no* sense of leadership from the shepherds! There simply must be complete and total surrender and submission to the shepherds if we are going to be moved into the truth that the Lord has for us!" Brother Wendall spoke fervently as I handed him a coke and a bag of chips I'd just bought from the vending machines.

"Well, I think I see what you mean, but could you explain further?" I asked. I actually didn't see at *all* what he was trying to say. He might as well have been speaking another language. Maybe the devil was again at work in my head, keeping me from understanding a deeper level of truth.

"The body in Mobile, Alabama under Brother Charles, one of the wisest of the shepherds, is completely in order and fully submitted as a congregation of the Lord should be if they want to hear from God." Brother Wendell swigged down his coke in nearly one gulp before slamming it down onto the table.

"There are other charismatic groups in Florida and prayer fellowships going on all around Mobile. Of course they are not yet included in the worship services because their ears are not yet ready for the full truth of the Lord. But they are learning to submit to their own shepherds and in the fullness of time; they will all be brought together as one." Brother Wendall smiled as he brought one fist into the air for emphasis. "I think the Lord will be helping me to make arrangements soon for our own body to visit the one in Mobile so they can see how much discipline they are lacking." Brother Wendall concluded rubbing his chin in thought.

Our break was swiftly over and throughout the rest of my day, I couldn't help but hope that we would not loose the spontaneity and joy of the high praises I'd come to love so dearly. I hadn't heard anything about that in Brother Wendall's vision for the future of the body here in Biloxi.

"Oh Lord, please show me soon who my own shepherd is to be! And Lord, I sure wouldn't mind if it was brother Wendall." I added quietly, hoping it would be. After all, he exuded the kind of confidence I'd always lacked and the wisdom which I so desperately desired. I'd tried to emulate his natural way with people on the sales floor. My sales records had perked up, however, so had everyone else's with the rapid approach of Christmas.

"Christmas!" I said out loud, smiling to myself. Surely this Christmas would surpass and outshine all the ones in the past, since this was the very first one in which I knew the Lord as a born again Christian!

However, an ominous sense of foreboding was ebbing its way into my mind, and seemed to be an ever present cloud throughout the day. Thus the need to make my way into the privacy of the back stockroom increased. I would plead the blood of Jesus and rebuke Satan numerous times back there before composing myself and returning to the sales floor, hopefully un-noticed.

While on the floor of the boy's department where I worked, the voices of customers and co-workers blended together, in a non-sensible singsong melody. I closed my eyes and dreamed of Sunday night service at the Farm.

"Lord, help me make it to Sunday night! I just know that there is healing waiting for me when I can lose myself in your high praises! Please Lord, let it come quickly!" I used my handkerchief to wipe the perspiration from my brow.

"Dave, let's have lunch together today, ok?" A friendly voice called to me over the rack of suits from the fragrance counter. It was Mrs. Jones, an ever-friendly older lady who liked to joke with everyone.

"Oh, um, well sure, but I was going now. Is that ok with you?" I asked, half hoping to myself she would not be able to make it. Today had been an especially anxious day for me and I really wanted nothing more than a quiet lunch where I could hide away and read my Bible which I proudly brought underneath my arm each morning as I came into work. I thought that toting the Bible around was one more silent way to witness to these poor, lost folks I worked with.

"Yeah, I'm ready when you are kiddo!" Mrs. Jones called out happily as she smacked her gum, scratching her beehive hairdo with a shiny long, red fingernail.

"C'mon, we're goin' to see the zoo!" Mrs. Jones grabbed me by the arm and marched me toward the mall entrance.

"Uh, there's no zoo here, Mrs. Jones." I said, thinking she must be a bit confused. Maybe the thick mascara she wore like a spider web was making her see things!

"Oh yeah, there's a great zoo here and I can get us some front row seats. You'll love it. Now c'mon and let yourself go a little Davie boy." Mrs. Jones said as she patted my arm. "That's right. Now, for the next hour, you and I are gonna forget about life's problems and just enjoy the view. Sit down right here. This will do just fine and dandy." Mrs. Jones said sitting down under the large palm tree by the giant water fountain in the center of the mall.

"Ok, I'm a bit confused Mrs. Jones. I don't see any signs of a zoo." I said looking ahead, straining to see anything that might remotely resembled a zoo.

"Oh you'd be surprised at all the animals you can see at this zoo, if you just open your eyes and look. Oh you see, right over there Dave? Now that's just about the brightest peacock I ever laid eyes on! What do you think?" Mrs. Jones slapped her knee and snorted as she covered her mouth. Straight ahead was a tall woman strutting proudly toward us wearing a neon bright orange and purple blouse with a bright red-feathered hat.

"Good grief, I need sun glasses." I laughed in spite of myself. The proud woman strutted by as though she were going down a high fashion catwalk. Thankfully, she never noticed the two of us snickering out loud.

"Oh hang on Dave, just *hang* on, because I see there coming our way a French poodle dead ahead." Mrs. Jones tapped her feet as she giggled watching the stately woman decked out in a white fur jacket and hat along with white ankle boots. "Well ooh la-la!" Mrs. Jones said smiling. "I think we need some pop corn for this show." She said strolling to a nearby shop to buy a large popcorn and two Cokes.

"Here, let me get my wallet out." I started, but she put her hand on my arm to stop me.

"Don't worry about it. You can get it next time." She said. "Oh, uh oh . . . . now look at that hippo!" Nearly unable to contain herself, she had to look the other way as the huge, dark skinned man decked out in a black trench coat approached, his large face sullen and serious.

"Hungry hippo, hungry hungry hippo!" I echoed the commercial which we'd all heard, looking at Mrs. Jones.

"Oh no, stop it! It hurts!" She said grabbing her stomach. "Well don't look now, but someone let the goat out of the pen." I added nodding toward an old hunched over gentleman with a goatee similar to the Kentucky fried chicken sign.

The lunch hour sped by and I found that my entire body felt kind of relaxed and lighter throughout the rest of the workday. Even my headache had lifted and I felt no urgent need to run to the stock room for emergency intercessory prayer time. I was very grateful to this gifted, fun-loving lady, albeit a common sinner, for helping to lighten my load this day. To my amazement, the Lord had moved even through a non-born again heathen. I would be sure to include Mrs. Jones in my prayer time this evening. Oh how wonderful it would be to see her brought over to the right side! Although she had mentioned being a long time member of a local denominational church, I was sure that no real truth could have possibly been taught there.

Christmas came and went with hardly a ripple of difference in my day-to-day existence. I thought surely this year would be extra special, but I'd been deeply disappointed on every level.

It was New Year's Eve and I found myself dragging off for another day's work at the mall with my usual dull headache and that strange, foreboding feeling that something was badly wrong with me. Where was my Christian joy? What had happened to the lighthearted days of fun with Cindy, Paul, and Cathy, all of whom now seemed to spend more time fasting and crying before the Lord than anything else. Cindy had suggested that we were all going through a 'valley'.

"Psst! Psst! Hey Dave, you hit the break room yet?" Mrs. Jones said leaning over the cosmetics counter smacking her gum happily. "You gotta try that punch the boss brought in for us! It's got all sorts of goodies in it, sure to give you a boost!"

"No, I haven't made it there yet, but I'm past due for my break." I answered putting down the box of boy's shirts I'd been tagging for the New Year's sale.

"Well c'mon then, my boy! It's time for a little pick-me-up!" Mrs. Jones giggled and came around the counter to go with me to the break room. Normally bleak and gray, the room now was festooned with brightly colored balloons hanging from the ceiling and crepe paper streamers draping downward. There was a large table decked out with a paper tablecloth proclaiming a Happy New Year to one and all, the table being loaded with homemade goodies. Right in the middle of the table was a beautiful glass punch bowl, with little cups hanging around the rim.

"See, what did I tell you, huh? Well go on! Don't be shy! Go get a cup full!" Mrs. Jones pushed me toward the bowl while she used the dipper to fill a cup for the both of us. A huge block of pink ice floated on top of the deep red, fruity smelling elixir.

"Mmm, this is good." I said quickly gulping down the entire glass. "Well go on and have another. That's what it's there for. Oh and have some of these little devil's food sandwiches too!" Mrs. Jones prepared a plate full of food for me, with loads of salty nuts. The sweet, cold punch washed down the nuts, leaving a warming sensation on its path downward. After the third cup was drained, I noticed that the throbbing in my head had completely evaporated. I had the strangest sensation of peace on earth and good will toward all men!

"Oh, hello Prunella." Mrs. Jones said, her smile fading from her red painted lips.

"Mrs. Jones; David." Prunella Grimsly nodded; her stern face a reflection of her equally dour spirit. Since the time I'd worked here, I only noticed her wearing two different colors, black and gray.

"Prunella, have some of that punch. It'll put a pucker in your pout!" Mrs. Jones said smiling, a snort escaping her lips without her intention.

Prunella Grimsley poured herself a dipper full of the concoction, bringing it slowly to her pursed bluish, gray lips, and then spewing it from her mouth, clasping her large, veiny hand to her withered bosom. "SPIKED! This vile, wicked juice shall not defile *my* body!" Mrs. Grimsley proclaimed loudly. She held the cup as far away from her as her long, thin arm would allow and proceeded to stomp toward the sink, the heels from her two inch buckle on shoes hammering loudly on the hard linoleum floors. The glass was held high in the air as the small amount of liquid splashed into the metal sink.

"This is typical of you Mrs. Jones, but David, I must say I'm deeply disappointed to see you sitting there so smug!" Prunella spun around on her heels and loudly marched from the break room.

"Oh she's just upset because someone dropped a house on her sister, wicked old witch that she is!" Mrs. Jones said before erupting into laughter.

I found myself laughing in spite of myself. Old Mrs. Grimsley really was quite "bound up" in her spirit and needed releasing from her old and all too traditional religiosity!

Deep down, I knew that someone had spiked the punch, but since no one had said anything to me about it, I didn't "officially" know. Therefore, it didn't really count! I had one more glass before happily returning to my daily routine, which didn't seem to be such a drudge. For the very first time in a while, I went the rest of the day without so much as the first demon bothering me.

I realized later that night, I had not made a single trip to the back stockroom to rebuke the devil. I drifted off to a peaceful sleep that night, with a slight smile on my face. The old song I'd learned in grade school was running through my head:

> "Camp town ladies sing this song, doo dah, doo dah.
> Camp town racetrack five miles long, oh the doo dah day!
> I come down south with my hat caved in, doo dah, doo dah.
> I go back home with a pocket full of tin, oh the doo dah day!
> Gonna run all night! Gonna run all day!
> I'll bet my money on the bob-tail nag, somebody bet on the grey!"

After my New Year's Day festivity, the return to the drudgery of work continued, along with the headaches and anxieties of the constant attack of Satan all through the day. My only relief was the hope of good services at the fellowship. I lived from service to service. It was my only lifesaver. The Sunday night services had recently been switched to Saturday night, though. Brother Wendall had announced the need for believers to attend their usual church in order that they might find common ground, thereby winning them over to the Spirit filled life.

This Saturday night service was to be the first in which both my Aunt Clarice and my mother would be attending. They had both visited some local spirit filled prayer groups during the week, so they should now be ready for what the House of Praise had to offer in truth and spirit. Cathy and I never felt the need to attend the local prayer groups. After all, why should we? We had found the full gospel at the fellowship. Any place else would just be a mere imitation of what God had intended for us. Our Daddy was still attending St. Thomas and my mother begrudgingly went along with him, but we remained in prayer for him that he would no longer be blinded by such false doctrine.

As soon as I arrived at the House of Praise for services, Dean saw me as I came inside and he greeted me warmly.

"Brother Dave! How's it going man?" He said with a smile and patting me on the back.

"Not so good. Satan has been buffeting me constantly and my head is really killing me right now." I said putting my hand to my forehead.

"I rebuke you Satan in the name of Jesus. I demand that you go back to the pit of hell from whence you came!" Dean said in a strong voice as I raised my hands in praise.

"Now just resist the temptation to give in to any symptoms he throws on you Dave!" Dennis said patting my back. I shook my head in agreement, willing myself to ignore the ever present strange sense that all was not well with me.

Someone started the singing with "Clap your hands all ye people, shout unto God with a voice of triumph!" Dean and I joined in together as I spotted my Aunt Clarice, Mama, and Cathy coming into the main room of worship. Before long, they seemed to be joining right along, raising their hands and clapping as though they had done this all their lives.

The service seemed to fly by and my headache lifted with the high praises that were sung in glorious harmony to the Lord, my sister's soprano voice weaving and blending in perfectly in her own praises to Jesus. At the close of services, I made my way over to my Aunt and Mother. Cathy had already flitted off somewhere speaking with some of the younger men from the Air Force base.

"Oh Dave this was great!" Aunt Clarice said raising her hands, a smile all across her face. "We're coming back, huh Ider?" She said putting her free arm around her sister.

"Oh, yeah, we'll be back. Just gotta pray for Gene!" Mama said gritting her teeth.

"Oh mercy sakes alive. Let's not mention him right now. We had too much fun to come down thinking about Gene!" Aunt Clarice said laughing.

"Dave, you and Cathy come home early now, ya hear?" Mama said as they headed toward the door.

"Yes M'am." I added, making my way over toward Cathy, Cindy and Paul. It was about time to head over to the local pizza place and enjoy our Saturday night socializing after services.

The following day after lunch, while in my room studying the Bible, I heard a firm knock at my closed bedroom door. Before having time to answer the knock, Daddy opened the door and came in, looking around as though taking in the feeling of my sanctuary.

"Dave, I'm coming next service you have at that glory to God place, with Mama." Daddy announced proudly shaking his head up and down, waiting for my approval.

"Well, that's good." I answered quietly, happy that my Father was finally submitting to the Holy Spirit who had no doubt been convicting him.

"Yeah, I think it's high time too. I want to get in on those, what do you call them 'lofty praise'?" He said, trying to be up on the spiritual lingo.

"*High* praises Daddy. They're called high praises." I answered a bit irritated that he had not remembered the correct term or even the right name of the place, for that matter.

That Saturday evening while mingling with friends before services began, I caught a glimpse of my father through the corner of my eye. Brother Wendall spotted him and immediately honed in. The two seemed as though they had known one another all their lives. Within moments I heard peals of laughter from both my dad and Brother Wendall.

I casually sauntered a bit closer so that I could hear some of the conversation. My curiosity was peaked and I wondered what these two could possibly have in common. Both were polar opposites of one another, like night and day!

"Oh Gene, your wisdom is rare these days! Where I come from in Pennsylvania, the work on the farm had to be done in the mornings before we left for school or for our jobs in town! We milked the cows, slopped the hogs, fed the chickens and livestock, and had to haul water to our mother to heat on the stove for washing the clothes!" Brother Wendall said. "Today's kids know nothing of such honest, hard work! They're spoiled beyond belief and it's the ruination of this country is what!"

"That's just exactly what I believe brother Wendall! I'll tell you one thing . . ." Daddy added shaking his finger.

"What's that brother Gene?" Brother Wendall hung on my father's every word, and '*brother* Gene'? How on earth did Daddy achieve that status just by talking about his favorite subject, "hard times"?

"This country is heading for another great depression and *no one* is going to know how to survive it!" Daddy added nodding his head upward.

"You took the words right out of my mouth brother Gene! Right now I'm trying to impress upon the younger brethren the importance of knowing basic survival skills such as gardening and raising chickens. Why the young women don't even know how to preserve foods! It's really a national disgrace! I think God wants his people to survive the upcoming days of tribulation!" Brother Wendall leaned in as though speaking in confidence only to my father about this subject of national importance.

How could Brother Wendall have possibly known the one subject that was nearest and dearest to my father's heart? He certainly had no way of perceiving that my father had lectured on that subject ad-nauseum! The terms "hard times are coming" had been used with abundant frequency ever since I could remember.

After discussing this with Cathy on the ride home, we both decided that the Lord was using Brother Wendall to win our father over. It seemed to have worked because he became a regular fixture at the House of Praise and was deeply impressed with brother Wendall. Those two had certainly hit it off!

Meanwhile, the attacks of the devil seemed to be ever increasing, especially while at work, prompting me to decide to speak with the elders at the fellowship about casting more demons out. Sister Parker had been forbidden to come to the House of Praise by her husband, and staying within submission to him, she honored his wishes. Sister Dolly still came to the Saturday evening services, but also attended her regular church services on Sunday mornings with her husband and family.

Paul had told me that the pastor there was Spirit filled and that Brother Wendall was even planning to bring a vanload of folks from the fellowship to visit. I was delighted when one day while at my job, that van stopped in front of the mall and the folks came into the store for a visit. My face lit up at the sight of my friends, Dean and Larry, who lightheartedly fumbled and played with some of the merchandise, making jokes that a corkscrew was a portable demon remover.

I was nearly rolling with laughter by the time they made their exit. When they left, it felt as though the daylight had been sucked out of the building and the clouds of my sadness immediately returned. I counted down the minutes until I could clock out of this mortuary and hot foot it to Paul's church to be with my friends!

I arrived a bit late and could hear the faint sound of singing coming from the sanctuary; "Come buy without money". It sounded all at once both comforting and foreign. I'd not heard actual hymns being sung in quite some time. As I walked into the sanctuary, the look and feel was quite similar to that of St. Thomas, my old church. It felt a bit awkward, but the sight of Paul, brother Wendall, Larry and Dean bolstered my spirit. I sat down as near to them as the crowd would allow, and listened to the sermon, which was delivered with much reverence and humility. After the end of the service when I passed by the pastor and brother Wendall who were deep in conversation, I heard the words, "door to Long Beach" being bantered about with much seriousness.

At the next service at the fellowship, brother Wendall pulled me aside as soon as I arrived in the back kitchen door.

"Brother Dave, there you are! I've just been discussing an important topic with some of the more mature brethren. I'm planning a small trip over to Mobile. That's where Brother Charles, a magnificent shepherd who has been used by the Lord to bring several of the local prayer groups together to form the body of Christ in the Mobile area leads his flock. I think it's of the utmost importance that the brethren here learn the discipline and honor that the disciples of the Lord show to the elders and leaders of the church. It's so needed here at the Farm! This church has been completely set in order!" Brother Wendall said, his brown eyes piercing into mine, showing me the magnitude of this issue.

"Well that all sounds good to me." I said thoughtfully; glad to be included among the "mature" brethren. "When do we go?"

"Now David, you must keep this to yourself! Don't even tell your sister or your parents. I don't think they are ready for these truths quite yet. We plan on taking our van over there next Saturday. I'm going to announce this Saturday that there will be no services here that night so that our elders are tutored by the Lord in some critical matters. I won't accept questions. This is a mandate!" Brother Wendall said tightening his lips and raising his eyebrows. I didn't think anyone would dare question his authority! I certainly wouldn't!

I got special permission from the store manager to get off of work early so that I might attend this most special event in Mobile. My excitement built all week within my heart as I imagined a service that would parallel the worship of all the angels in heaven!

The ride in the van was joyful as Paul and I sang worship choruses. He had brought along his guitar and was wearing his four-inch horse nail cross that was tied around his neck with a simple rope. It looked so disciple-like. The talk among the elders and brethren was in high expectancy of the revelations that we all might take away from Mobile and institute within the body of Christ at the House of Praise. This would truly be a momentous occasion! I wondered how many times we would reach the very pinnacle of worship, the ultimate high praise.

The building was an old Baptist church which had been purchased by this congregation. We all took our seats at the back of the church with much anticipation among us. The faces of the brethren all wore broad smiles, contrasted by the faces of the elders and brother Wendall, which were quite somber. The music leader stepped behind the podium and ordered everyone to turn to page 613.

"This must be a warm up for the real thing, Dave. I can hardly wait!" Paul whispered, fingering his huge cross while I fumbled for the page in the hymnal which we shared.

The older hymn, which was unknown to Paul or me, was sung without very many folks raising their arms in freedom and worship as I was used to seeing at the fellowship. The next song was a very old chorus, which was sung in similar fashion to the hymn. Several older choruses and hymns were sung following small breaks of silence in between.

"Ok, we must be warming up for the real climax of high praises." I whispered to Paul and he quietly shook his head in agreement. But the high praises never came. The singing was immediately followed by young men and women, dressed in old-fashioned looking clothing, performing short acting skits. Even though no denomination was mentioned, the performers clearly represented the Pentecostal or Holiness religious groups.

As the dramas were acted out, the people who were obviously portraying the traditional denominations and especially the Pentecostals were always the brunt of ridicule, showing them as though they normally bullied others that weren't like them, such as young women wearing skirts that were a bit above the knee, or young men with longer hair. Their religiosity was exposed, showing the need to find common ground with the younger converts rather than forcing old fashioned, bound up rules upon them. If this had been a game of darts, then these Pentecostals and old fashioned traditionalists were the target, and the arrows found their mark in the bull's eye! The humor was accepted wholeheartedly by the entire congregation who laughed uproariously throughout, proving to all that they, the more mature brethren, most certainly understood the deeper meaning behind the skit. Only well disciplined people in a non-traditional setting could truly be used in expanding the Kingdom of God.

At long last, the pastor of the flock took his place proudly at the podium.

"Open your Bibles brethren to 1 Corinthians 4:16." He said rocking back and forth on his heels, impatiently waiting for all the flickering of pages to cease.

"Wherefore I beseech you, be ye followers of me". He slammed his Bible closed and looked sternly at the congregation for a long pause before asking the question:

"Of who?" Again, he rocked back and forth on his feet, his upper lip stiff while his jaw worked furiously.

"Of me!" One of the elders shouted out from his seat. "That's right Brother! You are listening to the instruction of the Lord God Jehovah this night and I implore all of you who have ears to HEAR! You are to follow your own shepherd! Tonight, I have been placed by God Almighty to enlighten you to His holy word. If you do not follow your shepherd with complete and total surrender and obedience, you might as well spit in the face of our Lord and go follow the devil, like so many other heathens and even un-learned charismatics, who only *think* they are following the Lord!" The pastor stepped back from the podium and crossed his arms across his chest.

"Amen!" shouted the same elder as before. This was followed by a chorus of hallelujah's and thank you Jesus's. He had this congregation in his back pocket. However, for some reason, the little song; "I have decided to follow Jesus" kept floating through my brain. The idea of following man rather than following Jesus somehow did not sit right with me. I forced those thoughts from my mind so that I could continue to hear the message being taught.

"Brethren, I'm here to tell you that the crux of the issue is this: Through your continual and unquestioning discipleship, and *only* through your surrender to your shepherd, could you possibly become the *door* that God will use to bring the kingdom of God to Mobile!" The pastor again stepped back from the podium, his head erect, his upper lip dotted with beads of perspiration.

"After these new creatures in Christ have been properly discipled throughout the area in smaller prayer groups, then they will be prepared to worship here . . . . with the more *mature* brethren who are now ready for the meat of God's holy word and not just the milk! Milk is for babies! Meat is for *men*! "He removed his handkerchief and dotted it across his face before moving closer to the microphone and leaning onto the podium. "God's church *will* be without spot or wrinkle before you will be allowed to usher in the coming kingdom to this earth!" He raised his fist high into the air in a climax of the service.

"Amen and Amen!" the same elder echoed loudly.

Let us end this service with an appropriate song: "We are Marching to Zion!" The hymn was sung with gusto. As I looked across the faces of the brethren, I noticed not one smile crossed the lips of a single person.

That night, once again, all was not well with my soul. I slept in fitful spurts where giant demons chased me through every corner of hell. I rebuked them in the name of Jesus, my mouth trying to form the name of my precious Lord and savior, but my voice and words were slurred!

As dawn slowly broke and a beam of light found its way into my dark little room, I threw back the covers, knelt by my bed and went through every regimen I had learned to rebuke the devil. I even got out one of my little faith pamphlets and repeated the words of the page out loud, hoping to find some relief. I was surely being buffeted by the dreadful hounds of hell. Plans were made in my mind to speak with Brother Wendall at my very soonest opportunity to let him know that I must surely still have some demons that needed to be cast out. I just must find the peace of God once more which every other person at the House of Praise already had.

CHAPTER 5

THROUGH THE NIGHT

Yeah, though I walk through the valley
Of the Shadow of Death
I will fear no evil for Thou art with me
Thy rod and thy staff, they comfort me (Psalm 23:4)

The short, cold and dreary days of February had arrived. The deep purple sunset was in my rear view mirror as I drove directly from work to the weekly meeting at the House of Praise. A cold chill gripped me as I shivered, grasping the icy cold steering wheel.

"C'mon heat! Surely you can do better than that!" I said as I switched the blower to high and moved the dial all the way into the red-hot zone. "Ahh, that's better." I replied as though the car could hear me giving it orders and compliments. Just then a horn honked from the car behind me. I could see my parents and Cathy in my rear view mirror as they drove along, on their way to the fellowship as well.

The inseparable Cindy and Karla would no doubt be going in their own car, possibly with Paul hitching a ride. He wouldn't miss a meeting and would ride with his mother or Cindy and Karla. Cathy had no choice but to ride with our parents because neither Karla nor Cindy would have anything to do with her unless I was involved in some way. They completely shut her out although I couldn't quite understand why. Cathy was certainly popular enough with all the rest of my friends, especially the fellows.

I looked forward to seeing the folks at the fellowship. Just the thought of them helped to ease the sense of anxiety and sometimes rapid thoughts filled with panic. These same attacks from Satan now seem to have been going on for an unendurable amount of time. Sometimes the oppression was so overwhelming that I felt as if I could no longer function. My body was constantly exhausted from fighting. The struggle took place not only all day long, but also throughout many sleepless nights. My only relief seemed to come during the worship time at the House of Praise. I needed the fellowship meetings as I needed the very air I breathed! Maybe, the service tonight would help rid me of the demons that tormented me!

"Oh David, how's the headache tonight?" I heard the distinct Pennsylvania Dutch accent come from sister Dolly who had taken a very motherly concern to my misery. The only way I could describe the suffering I went through was to call it a headache. "You know I've had those sinus headaches a lot here lately. I think it's just all this humidity we've been having lately. I never had them in Pennsylvania!"

"Well, I don't think these are from the humidity, sister Dolly." I quietly answered. "I'm hoping for some relief soon though, maybe in the high praises." I tried to force a smile, though the corners of my mouth felt stiff and heavy.

"I'm praying for you Dave." Sister Dolly said patting my shoulder. "Brethren, let's sing a song of praise to our Lord!" Brother Wendall said in his booming voice raising his hands upward. The entire room stopped their chattering and began clapping and singing the familiar upbeat chorus; Clap Your Hands All Ye People.

I commanded my heavy arms upward in praise to God, feeling nothing but tired and guilty for my lack of enthusiasm. "Thank you Jesus. Praise you Jesus. I rebuke you Satan in the name of Jesus." I chanted. I could feel tears stinging the corners of my eyes. It was as if the joy had been completely drained dry from my soul. My spirit grieved and ached for the presence of the Lord, to *feel* the same peace within that once had permeated my heart and mind.

All through the service I forced myself to join in, but still, the flow of God's love had been cut off, or so it seemed. This had to be the veil of Satan attempting to trick me! I determined then and there to speak with brother Wendall after service. He would advise me about how to get deliverance once and for all!

The message was preached with the same fervor as ever and the joy from the brethren surrounding me only served to remind me of the lack I was feeling within. The final closing song was sung and I immediately made my way directly for Brother Wendall.

"David, praise the Lord Brother! How are you?" Brother Wendall patted me on the back firmly.

"Well, I need to talk to you about just that." I said looking him directly in the eyes.

"Ok, share with me the burden of your heart." Brother Wendall's face became serious.

"It's these headaches and the nightmares and daily anxiety attacks, Brother Wendall. They absolutely dominate my every waking moment! Sometimes I think I can't make it through another day like this! I've just got to have deliverance from these demons! No matter how I try to gain the victory over this, I'm living in defeat. I know the only possible reason for this is demonic!" I said in desperation.

Brother Wendall's face became serious as he pondered the situation. Then the light of an idea flickered across his face. "David when is your next day off?"

"Wednesday." I responded quickly; hope already beginning to soar within me.

"Ok, you come out here Tuesday night and stay the night. I'll speak with Ron and Andy who have the ministry of casting out demons. Be sure to be in a state of fasting and prayer! Everything will be done strictly in order, I assure you! Then Wednesday, you can come with me on some visits I have to make in the town of Leakesville. It's such a quaint little town and there is great need there for a door." Brother Wendall said seriously.

"Yeah, that'd be good! I'll be here right after I get off work, thanks!" I said as the first smile I'd felt crease my face in days forced my mouth into the unfamiliar shape of a natural smile.

"See you then David." Brother Wendall said smiling down at me with his magnetic grin.

"Hey Davey boy! Is it time for pizza or what, man?" Paul called out from across the room.

"Ok, I'm coming. Where's Cathy?" I asked.

"She's over there talking with Brother Larry. She said to tell you not to leave without her because your parents have already gone. Hey come to think of it, so have mine, man! I need to hang a ride with you two." Paul said smiling his goofy smile as he walked across the room in his loud striped pants, his large cross made from nails swinging back and forth with each step. His grin was nearly invisible from his bushy mustache that covered his top lip.

"Hey Paul, you can ride with us!" Cindy called out happily.

"I'll ride with you Cindy!" Cathy answered nearly skipping over to the growing circle.

"There won't be room Cathy, sorry." Cindy answered curtly.

"Ok brother, you're stuck with me. I guess it's just us two again." Cathy said, her face showing the sting of Cindy's rejection.

"No, it'll be us three." Paul said throwing his arm around Cathy playfully.

"C'mon Cindy. We can just meet them there." Karla grabbed Cindy by the arm as they spun around to leave quickly, whispering as they strode together arm and arm.

"Hey I'll follow in my car too if that's ok?" Larry asked.

"Sure man, the more the merrier!" Paul answered.

Larry had recently been discharged from the Air Force for reasons unknown to me. Now he lived at the House of Praise. I couldn't help but envy him. I could just envision myself living in this peaceful setting where everyone got along and praised the Lord together all the time. Surely Satan couldn't come near me in such a place as this. Everyone was Spirit filled!

Tuesday

February 5th, 1974

The clock on the wall at work seemed to tick by at an agonizingly slow pace this day. There had only been a handful of customers all day long and the place felt like a tomb. My emotions swung back and forth from excited anticipation to mortal fear and dread.

I fasted through my lunch hour and strolled through the mall, looking but not seeing anything in the store windows. I remembered the Tuesday night services at the Farm, which brother Wendall had stopped in favor of home Bible studies to be held in each town across the coast. Because Sister Parker was in submission to her husband, the studies at her home had ceased, leaving me bereft of any fellowship and worship during the week. I lived from Saturday night to Saturday night. Most everyone had been given the word from the Lord as to who their shepherd was to be. I had not yet received that word. Perhaps tonight would be the night that Brother Wendall would reveal the good news to me that he would be my personal shepherd!

I couldn't clock out and get to my car fast enough. With trembling hands I cranked up the car, my overnight bag already prepared and sitting in the seat beside me. I set out on the now familiar path, down winding country roads to the fellowship. The very sight of the house on this cold night as my car crunched the oyster shell driveway gave me a sense of peace. The camellia bushes were the only color that dotted the brown winter lawn that stretched all the way down to the peaceful lake. This place had become my haven.

"Hey there Brother Dave, come on in." Larry greeted me at the back door of the old farmhouse kitchen. I'm just having some toast, you want a piece?" Larry, donned in an un-tucked flannel shirt was at ease with the world it seemed.

"No Larry, Brother Dave has business to attend to with the Lord this night which doesn't include eating earthly manna." Brother Wendall said; his lips tight as he reached out to guide me to an office I'd never been in before.

Both Brother Andy and Brother Ron were already seated around an old rather beat up, large wooden desk with only a simple oil lamp and a large Bible adorning the top. The little office was lined with bookshelves; old dusty books from the owners of the house had been left behind and obviously never touched. The dark little room had an eerie glow as the oil lamp flickered and spit out the small amount of light, just enough to see the faces of the men in the room. Brother Wendall quietly crept out, closing the old creaking door behind him.

"Just have a seat Brother Dave." Andy offered. "We've been in prayer and fasting this day and are prepared to do battle with the devil on your behalf this evening. Brother Ron, do you want to fill Brother Dave in on what is to take place?"

"Yes, I think that would be in order. I'll be starting the service with the reading of some scriptures. God will be here, providing a hedge of protection from the evil one throughout the night. We will then begin to command the demon to manifest itself and give us its name. It's vital that we know the name of the evil one before casting it out to the pit of darkness." Brother Ron leaned forward into the light, the creases in his forehead becoming deeper as he lifted his hand before continuing. "There could be more than one, Brother, so we want you to know that we will be here as long as it takes to have you completely clean so the Holy Spirit can come and fill the void spaces. You don't want to have an empty space in your soul because that just invites the demon to come back in and it will then bring hordes more along with it!" Brother Ron leaned back in his chair, the light fading from his face as he did so.

I shook my head numbly. I could feel my teeth begin to chatter even though I was not in the least bit cold.

"Let's start out with a song of praise to the almighty King of Kings." Brother Andy lifted his hands and began to sing, "God is so good," Slowly, deeply, his eyes half closed, half-fluttering, he rocked back and forth gently. Brother Ron began to exalt the Lord as the three of us attempted to enter into high praises.

The praises felt as though they had been sung in a minor key, giving the song an unnatural and strange sound.

"Brethren of the Lord . . . . Let us begin." Brother Ron said looking directly at me as though he were preparing for war. I too had prepared to rid myself of this horrible evil that infested my soul!

"You foul spirit from the pit of hell, I command you to manifest yourself, in the name of Jesus!" Brother Ron shouted.

I had heard that on many occasions, the demons spoke out before they left, and words began to formulate in my mind. I heard myself give voice to these words as I felt them spit from my mouth.

"I don't want to leave!" I said. My body slumped forward and I heard my knees make a hollow thud onto the floors.

"What is your name evil one?" brother Ron once more commanded.

The word 'fear' swirled through my mind until there was room for nothing else inside my being.

"FEAR!" I shouted, my voice sounding raw from emotion. My entire being felt limp, completely consumed with misery and dread.

"You spirit of fear, I command you to come out now! In the name of Jesus, release Dave from your vice!" Brother Ron shouted.

Brother Andy came placing one hand upon my head and raising the other toward heaven, uttering prayers in unknown tongues. Sweat began to form above his brow as fervent prayers flowed from deep within.

"I don't want to come out!" I seemed to growl from deep within myself without power to control my own words.

"You will release him NOW!" Brother Ron's voice roared loudly.

"I renounce you foul spirit in the name of Jesus Christ of Nazareth!" I said coughing as tears flowed down my face, dropping onto the floor beneath me.

"Now GO evil one, to the deepest part of the ocean and never come back to torture this brother again!" Brother Ron and Andy now prayed in agreement together.

The three of us in that small room began to praise the Lord in unison. The burden on my soul, once heavy and dark as midnight, now lifted and the sun was shining once more. I could breathe!

The praises grew quieter and more reverent until each of us grew silent, opening our eyes. Both Brother Ron and Brother Andy reached down, helping me up off the floor and into my chair.

"Do you think they are all gone?" I asked quietly.

"Well, sometimes one or two of them can hide, but I feel reasonably assured that we got them all. There was a sense of victory in the air." Brother Ron said smiling. Brother Andy nodded in agreement.

"How do you feel Brother Dave?" Ron asked.

"Well, I feel much better than when I came in here. I can sense God's presence again." I answered. I could indeed feel the peace of the Lord flowing through me once more.

Just then there was a gentle knock at the door as Brother Wendell peeked in. "How are things going?" He asked.

"The Lord God is King and the devil has been cast into the pit of hell!" Brother Ron added.

"Praise the Lord!" added Brother Andy joyously.

"Yes, thank you Jesus." I added relieved that the ordeal was indeed over and the light of God was once more being felt from within.

"Now Brother Dave, you just remember when that ole devil comes around with his fear, you just repeat the 23rd Psalm, "Yea though I walk through the valley of the shadow of death, I will fear no evil for Thou art with me."

"Yes, I will remember." I added smiling weakly. "Ok, there's a bit of supper prepared out in the kitchen. Who's up for hot dogs tonight, huh?" Brother Wendall announced happily.

"Sounds good to me, let's go!" Brother Ron said heading toward the door. "Brother Wendall makes a mean German hot dog with lots of sauerkraut."

"Ugh, well, no not for me. I'm a mustard man myself." I said grinning sheepishly.

"Oh no Dave, you *must* have some good sauerkraut!" Brother Wendall insisted.

"No, no, thanks all the same." I answered.

Curiously, Brother Wendall continued to tease me and insist upon me trying the sauerkraut. Eventually he gave up the idea, seeing I had no intention of doing what I had called 'adventure eating'.

After supper, Larry and I took the dishes to the old white farmhouse sink and started to wash them together. He and I had formed a fond friendship and always enjoyed spending a little time with each other. Conversation flowed easily between us about any given subject.

"Hey Dave, do you remember an old late night radio program called Beeker Street? It was a syndicated show and they used to play the best music!" Gary said smiling whimsically.

"Yeah, I do remember that! I picked it up at night time on an AM station out of Little Rock, Arkansas. Man that was a long time ago!" I said, squinting my eyes and trying to pull up the old memories I had filed away in the dusty corners of my mind. "'Beeeeker Streeeet', they used to say in a creepy sounding voice." I waited for a response from Larry.

"A lifetime ago, back in the days when we were 'in the world'." Larryy said grinning while handing me a freshly washed plate.

"Yeah, the music was really cool, but kinda weird, too! All the kids used to talk about it on Monday mornings in school." I laughed and set the clean dried, white plate into the cupboard, noticing the pale green paint was badly chipping all about the edges of the door.

Just then brother Wendall happened to walk through the kitchen briskly. "You guys going back into the world?" He quipped and walked away quickly, not waiting for a response.

Larry and I looked at one another sheepishly and finished our task without further conversation. Brother Wendall had obviously been eavesdropping, or maybe he just happened upon our conversation innocently.

With the hour being late, everyone began to drift toward his appointed rooms for bedtime. I couldn't help but wonder which room would be mine when Brother Wendall placed his hand upon my shoulder in a friendly slap.

"You're bunking with me tonight Dave. I have some further counseling we must attend to." Brother Wendall said with a friendly pat on my back as he made his way toward the darkened staircase.

I wonder why I don't get my own room. Hmm, must not be an extra one available. Oh well, there's bound to be a couple of beds in brother Wendall's room. Perhaps he is going to tell me tonight that the Lord has shown him he is to be my spiritual shepherd and he wants to tell me in private! That has to be it!

The battered wooden steps creaked and groaned as I followed Brother Wendall to his room upstairs. I never even knew there were any bedrooms upstairs because all the brethren who lived here stayed in the rooms downstairs. I had been upstairs once before when some airmen were staying in a room that was akin to a bunkhouse with single bunk beds lining the walls and stacked two by two. Occasionally they visited and would stay in what was known as "the bunk wing".

The air smelled musty as though not much stirred in this area. The hallway was completely dark other than a thin beam of soft light that cut through the darkness. Brother Wendall followed that beam into what was his room. This wing was on the opposite end of the 'bunk wing'; completely desolate and left closed up. A small flutter rumbled through my stomach and up into my throat.

"Just set your things down on that chair." Brother Wendall said as he took his watch off and began to prepare for bed.

There was only one double bed in the small, dark room. I put my wallet and watch on the dark wooden chest of drawers nervously. I guess he will counsel with me quickly before sleeping I thought as I began to become a bit self-conscious.

"Here Dave, wear this tonight." Brother Wendall pulled two long white gowns out of the dresser drawer for both of us. "All the men and boys in Pennsylvania wear them Dave. We aren't so bound up as some of you folks down here." Brother Wendall said in a condescending manner. "There's absolutely no need for all those underclothes when you wear this simple gown." Brother Wendall slipped quickly into the white muslin gown taking off all of his underclothing and slipping into bed.

"Well, I guess I never, ugh." I stammered, uncomfortable with the foreign garment, but not wanting to show my ignorance to him.

"You know Dave, you simply have to let go of things and accept something that is actually better for you! Oh you are such a baby!" Brother Wendall said laughing at me.

"Ok, I guess you're right. It's just, sort of, different, that's all." I said quietly.

I slipped out of my undergarments in record speed so as not to draw attention to myself. The gown felt strange on my bare skin, but I assumed that at some point it might seem more comfortable. I only wanted to curl up and go to sleep as quickly as possible. Perhaps the 'counseling' could take place tomorrow morning. Who could possibly carry on a normal conversation wearing a get-up like this? I must really be bound up, to feel so uncomfortable.

I crawled into the bed and lay as close to the edge as possible, my only desire being to fall into a deep sleep soon. However Brother Wendall had other plans which obviously involved talking.

"Brother Wendall, I wish I knew who my shepherd was to be. I've been in prayer about it, but still, I've not yet been led in any certain direction. Is it you?" I was hoping the answer would be yes, but instead was shocked by his response.

"Why you don't know the answer to that simple question yet?" Brother Wendall asked incredulously. "Why that's the easiest question there is. It's your father, of course! A son is to submit to his father. That's the Biblical way, Dave and you have much that you could learn from him! Now that's he's joined us, he is most certainly meant to be your shepherd!"

I laid there in stunned silence. My father! How on earth was it that God meant for my father to be my shepherd? He was just about the most un-qualified leader I'd ever known when it came to spiritual matters. It was true he had attended a few meetings, but he had made no real changes yet in his daily life; not to mention the fact that he had not even made any sort of profession of faith in Christ as his personal savior. Everything I'd learned since becoming a born-again Christian demanded a conversion in all these areas! My head reeled with the thoughts of this outrageous idea.

"Now Dave, I know what you are thinking. 'Why must I submit to my father? I've known the Lord much longer than him! But, that's only your pride, now isn't it?' But you have to trust me in these matters because I'm a far more mature man of God and have made it my life to live in the Word! I know of what I speak! Really Dave, I thought you were ready for more than just the milk of God's word! You have to be mature to accept the meat! Now try to do some growing up." Brother Wendall demanded.

"Brother Wendall, have you ever heard of the Tanner's prayer group over in Pass Christian that meets each week in their home? It's a non-denominational meeting and I've heard it's really wonderful." I said anxious to change the subject.

"Yes! Carol Lero!" Brother Wendall said with peels of laughter. "She thinks she's the mighty prophetess! She's nothing but a rebel rouser and should be kept at home! Her time would be better spent learning how to bake better biscuits for her husband! Dave, the Tanners are nice enough, but you need to have some wisdom and learn to discern the groups that are living in rebellion. We have made changes around here to sift out those undisciplined charismatic groups." He said with a sniff.

It was true that many changes had been made to the House of Praise since I had joined its members and become one of the brethren. Most had not been to my liking, but then I did have to learn submission as a good Christian. I was trying so hard to mature, in the way that God would want me to! How was it that I seemed to be 'inhibited' as he was so fond of putting it?

"Hey Dave, I hope you don't mind me changing the subject here, but I've got an important question for you. I don't want you to take offense either." Brother Wendall had changed his tone to one of seriousness. "Tell me, when you're at work or most anywhere, have you ever been in front of a nice looking man, and found yourself attracted to him?"

"No, no never ever." I said somewhat dumbfounded, wondering where this kind of question had come from. Am I so green and unsophisticated?

"Not even when you look at young, handsome boys wearing tight jeans?" Brother Wendall said calmly. "How about anything else, you know what I mean?"

"I'm sure the answer would be no to all of your questions. Remember I was raised Catholic. I was taught that intimacy of all kinds was to be reserved for the sanctity of marriage only." I said in a curt manner hoping this would change the line of questioning.

However it continued, becoming more and more suggestive. As Brother Wendall continued to probe the most private areas of my life with his questions, it became evident even to me that he had crossed the line into forbidden territory. I never had been in any situation in my life such as this one and was completely ill equipped to handle it properly.

"Uh, I'm really tired and we have to get up early, so good night." I said sheepishly as I rolled over onto the corner of the bed and closed my eyes. The air was thick with tension for several long moments.

"Well, good night then." He said.

Just then I felt the weight of his arm pressing around me as he scooped me closer to him. My heart pounded within my chest as I froze in fear, forcing the words out of my mouth, first in a whisper and then louder and louder as his embrace became more demanding.

"No, NO NO!" I protested as he continued to clutch me, more tightly with each moment. I lay there in utter alarm and shock, unable to move. This can't be happening to me! I must be making this up!

"STOP, NO!" I said loudly this time, my heart pounded within my brain so hard I thought it would explode!

"Oh ok then! Gee! Such a baby! I'll leave you to your precious sleep then!" Brother Wendall said in disgust rolling over to his side of the bed.

I was unable to move either my arms or legs. I lay quietly still, hoping that all would be well and this would go away like a bad dream but soon, the nightmare returned. This time his arm locked me into his demanding embrace, leaving me utterly powerless to escape.

"NO, NO, NO!" I forced myself to speak the words as tears ran helplessly down my face and onto my pillow. I was unable to wrap my head around what was happening to me. This had to be a dream!

"STOP THIS! NO, NO!" I demanded as he continued to invade my privacy in a way in which I had never before even considered or knew anything of.

"Why do you keep saying that? I don't understand you Dave!" Sighing, he finally stopped and released his grip.

"I'll leave you alone. You don't have to worry about me attacking you in the night either. You have my word. Good grief, what a child you are!" He huffed angrily.

I lay there in terror until I heard the heavy breathing of sleep overtake him. I was safe now, I concluded. Should I get away and go home? But that would only force me into an uncomfortable conversation with my parents who would surely want to know why I had come home in the middle of the night. No, I couldn't face them. What on earth would I tell them? As all these matters raced through my exhausted brain, images of my father racing over here with a shotgun; blowing away everyone who lived here came to mind. My dad could become quite furious when it came to protecting his family. No, I could certainly not go home! I could tell no one! I'd have to hold this secret deep within and be careful never to betray the dark occurrence that haunted my soul.

Where could I go? What should I do? This had been the only place on earth I'd found peace and love and learned of God's word as I should have. I feasted upon the high praises like a starving child, desiring the touch of the Lord. If I left here, where else was there to go in order to achieve that feeling? How could I find a church that would even consider helping deliver me from the demons which constantly beset me? To leave now would be to walk away from the only true feelings of love and peace I'd ever known, from the very presence and light of God! I couldn't throw it all way.

What if he had not actually attempted this unspeakable deed after all? How could so many people have placed such utter and complete trust in this man if he were a phony?

Wanting and needing so desperately to believe in all the wonderful truths that God had shown me over these past several months, I tried to convince myself that this could not have happened and I worked hard to push it out of my mind altogether. It was true that I was green in all things pertaining to sexuality of any nature. Maybe this is something that men do and I just never knew of such things? But it felt wrong and I wanted no part of it!

"Oh Lord Jesus, how will I ever get through this?" I prayed over and over again as a tormented sleep finally overtook my exhausted body.

The cold gray light of morning spilled into the musty upper bedroom, awakening me from a night of tormented dreams. The sheet was twisted about my feet in evidence of the fitful sleep the night before.

Brother Wendall was already up and dressed with his back facing me as I quickly slipped into my clothes, hurrying so as to go unnoticed.

"Good morning Dave. Shall we offer a morning prayer of thanksgiving together?" Brother Wendall asked smiling as though nothing in the slightest was amiss. He seemed capable of pushing the event completely from his mind as though it had never taken place. What a gift!

"Sure." I said quietly bowing my head as brother Wendall instinctively took the lead.

"Lord we thank you for the morning before us and I ask forgiveness for any transgression I may have committed last night. I plead the blood of Jesus and trust that all is forgiven and forgotten, separated as far as the east is from the west. Please guide and lead us in our mission today to give glory to you in all things that we say and do, amen!" Brother Wendall said with a final handclap. It felt sort of like an episode of Bewitched, where you could clap your hands and something disappeared into thin air, magically!

The day passed by in a blur. Brother Wendall and I met with a kindly middle-aged woman in the small town of Leakesville. The woman felt intently that the Lord wanted her to facilitate the building of a full gospel church in her small town. She obviously put a great deal of confidence in Brother Wendall's opinion, having visited the House of Praise several times, but he continually shot her idea down saying "We have too many churches as it is, Sister. You just need to find a home Bible study which can be used as the door to Leakesville; thereby funneling them toward the House of Praise when they are mature enough to join in with the other brethren in true worship and praise.

It was all that I could do to hold myself together in one piece, as I felt I could very well be losing my sanity. My mind was wandering wildly and it took full concentration just to make common responses throughout the day. Being so wrapped up in what was consuming me, I was completely oblivious to the miracle of life which was taking place on the other side of town in a small hospital in Gulfport. My sister, Cherie, was giving birth to her first son, my nephew on this sixth day of February 1974.

After a long day we entered into the back door of the fellowship and Brother Ron told me I needed to call my Mom right away. She had apparently been calling all day and wondering where I was.

I could barely remember my own phone number, but managed to sound normal when Mama answered the phone.

"Hi Mama." My voice sounded foreign to me.

"Well Dave, I swan, where in this world have you been?" Without waiting for an answer or taking a breath, she continued. "I've been trying to get you all day long! Anyway, Cherie had her baby! It's a little boy with a head full of hair like a little monkey! Cute as a button and screams to beat the band! Cherie's fine, now you get yourself on home now ya here?" Mama finally took a breath.

"Yes mam." I responded and quickly hung up the old black phone upon the wall receiver.

I gathered my belongings, and made my way out of the door to my car quietly and quickly as though escaping the scene of a crime, not fully aware if I had spoken with anyone or not. I cranked my car and drove down the oyster shell drive to get away as quickly as possible.

"Lord, thank you for being with me. Now, please help me get home safely. I love you Lord! I rebuke you Satan and command you to leave my mind alone!" I repeated this mantra all the way home, struggling to keep it together.

The little green house on Linda Lane looked as though I'd not seen it in a very long time, perhaps a lifetime ago. I feasted my eyes on the innocence of it all. My nieces bicycle was parked in front of the shed, and the screened in porch with the worn rockers and picnic table were reminders of a stable environment. Did I live here? Could I have ever been this innocent?

"Hey hon, did you have a good time?" Mama asked setting the table for supper and smiling at me.

"Oh yes, it was good." I said unable to meet her inquisitive gaze. I darted to my room thinking I had just lied to my mother and now I would have to ask forgiveness from the Lord!

I shut the door to my bedroom, feeling unsolicited tears stinging my eyes and rolling down my face. The last time I'd slept in this bed, I was as innocent as a child. I slid to my knees and cried out to God in agony and desperation.

"Oh God in heaven, how in the world did this horrible thing happen to me? Please, please keep me from falling apart!"

The tears continued to flow as I took my shower, scrubbing myself repeatedly as though I had wallowed in the mud which needed to be severely scoured in order to wash it from my being.

I managed to make it through the suppertime meal without attracting any attention to myself. No one suspected anything. But how long could I continue this charade? I felt no assurance that I would ever make it out of this dark valley.

After supper, I went to my room to read my Bible and a tiny glimmer of hope invaded the darkness of my mind as I read the 23rd Psalm: "Yea though I walk through the valley of the shadow of death, I will fear no evil, for Thou art with me. They rod and Thy staff, they comfort me." I flipped through the pages, seeking further comfort when my eyes fell upon the last few verses in chapter 11 of Matthew. "For My yoke is easy, and my burden is light."

A wave of gentle peace blanketed itself about me as I began to realize that the Lord was not the author of heavy burdens. I allowed myself to rest through the night, knowing that God was still indeed with me.

CHAPTER 6

A FARM IN LONG BEACH

The gathering clouds in my mind had produced a dark depression within my soul. The long, idle days working in the clothing store at the Edgewater Mall became unbearable. I longed for the bright, fun days back at the old A & P grocery store with my friends where hours flew by with lighthearted banter accompanied by the constant influx of customers. After a brief talk with my old boss, he gladly welcomed me back to my former job and within days I found myself slipping back into the familiar and comfortable routine of bagging groceries and stocking shelves, with the occasional "zapping" of a paper wad stinging me in the back from the pranksters in the stock room. I was home.

My friend Larry at the House of Praise had slid right into the job I had left vacant at the mall. For the first time, I found myself feeling a bit sorry for him, rather than envying him. Only weeks before, I had so wished

I could be in his place, living at the fellowship among the Godly brethren. That wish had quickly flickered out, like a falling star on a winter's night.

I carried on as normally as possible for the next few weeks, forcing the awful dark night to the deep, dusty corners of my mind. I worshipped at the House of Praise as though nothing out of the ordinary had transpired. But the winds of change were sweeping through the fellowship. These unwelcome changes could be felt more than seen.

I had kept the odious secret to myself, telling no one. My dad and Brother Wendall had struck up a friendship which was based purely on their shared interest of "hard times coming" and other 'common ground' which Brother Wendall had found. My Dad had invited him and Brother Ron to the house for a home cooked meal. All the day long, we were busily making preparations, scrubbing everything within the home as though an operation were to take place rather than a family meal. Our house was always sparkling clean and certain principles were indoctrinated into all of us, such as the removal of one's shoes before entering. All of our shoes were neatly aligned on the front screened porch, which helped to keep the floors so clean you could eat off of them.

"Brother Wendall and Brother Ron, why come on in here!" My father beamed opening the screen door to the kitchen. Also accompanying them was Brother Price, an amiable man and proud owner of a local pawn shop. He was one of the only members of the House of Praise who attended with both his wife and two children. Whole families were somewhat of an anomaly at the believer's meetings.

"Oh my, what an orderly home you have here Gene! Just let me remove my shoes first!" Brother Wendall said as he quickly slipped off his shiny loafers. Brother Ron quickly followed his example.

"Oh now you don't have to do that!" My father bemoaned quickly. "Well that's the way we always did it on the farmhouses back in Pennsylvania! It's a habit and a good one! You know cleanliness is next to godliness! It would surely do this younger generation a world of good if they would hearken to the wisdom of these principles!" Brother Wendall said, coming into the kitchen looking around as though he were a lion half starved.

"Sister Ida, upon my word that smells wonderful, like a good home made stew I used to get back home!" Brother Wendall rubbed his belly with a look of avarice in his flashing brown eyes. I found myself wishing he'd go back to Pennsylvania.

"No, it's not a stew. It's a roast with potatoes and carrots. We got some cornbread to go with that and a homemade pear pie from the pears off of our own tree for dessert." Mama said as she started setting the table.

"Let's go ahead and get seated here brothers, it's time for supper!" My father led the way to his usual spot at the head of the table, which for tonight was much larger than usual due to the extra leafs that had been added for the special occasion.

"Brother Gene, it's good to see that you have such a useful helpmate and a well ordered family! You know folks around here could learn from you about planting their own pear trees for fruit and vegetables for gardens! There are dark times ahead and no one will be prepared!" Brother Wendall warned everyone with a low voice.

"I've always said the same thing, but no one wants to listen! In hard times you take what you can get and are d'uhh, well, darned thankful for it!" My father said catching himself before the profanity had escaped.

"Oh Gene, that is so true! You know Long Beach needs a door . . . . a door to the kingdom and you could very well be that door!" Brother Wendall said, then quickly looked down at the huge helping of food my mother had just placed before him.

"There ya go. A big boy like you needs a good hot meal!" My mother said. She was in her element.

"Uh, brother Gene, it's only right that the head of the house lead the rest in a prayer of thanksgiving for this bounty." Brother Wendall commented seriously to my father, who instantly sat even straighter in his chair, his teeth clenched tightly as seriously as a man going into battle.

My father straightened up about six inches taller as his chin jutted forward. "Well then, uh, ok." He said with a sniff, his head bobbing an affirmative reaction without his knowledge. "Lord God, it's in your name we thank you for this food, and the gifts we are about to receive, from Thy bounty, through Christ our Lord, Amen." He said, ending the prayer which was not surprisingly almost identical to the Catholic one he had prayed all his life. I'd never heard any other blessing come out of his mouth in my life.

"Amen and Amen, Brother Gene!" Brother Wendall said, his fork already poised to dive into his supper. After gulping down nearly half his plate in a matter of seconds, the conversation took a familiar turn . . . . the apocalypse.

"You know a good bit of this food we are eating here tonight either came from our garden or from the fruit trees on this lot." My father boasted. "I think it's important to be self sufficient in these days. People think they can just go to the store or to McDonald's to get food, but they'd all like as not starve to death if they had to do without in hard times!" My father said with a tone that was getting as wound up as a corkscrew.

"As the brethren have heard me say on many occasions!" Brother Wendall said, pounding the table so loudly with his fist that the silverware rattled.

"Why that's right. Just on the way over here, Brother Wendall was talking about raising peeps and having a garden." Brother Price added with Ron nodding in agreement.

"Brother Gene, you and I are on the same wave length! Why people today are so spoiled and so deluded . . . why they'd be knocking on your door *begging* for food one day when the end times come and there are no stores for them to go to!" Brother Wendall stated with wide-eyed enthusiasm. It was like throwing gas on a fire. The rest of the meal and throughout the clean up process was consumed with talk of nothing but hard times and how the rest of the world would rue the day they didn't listen to the wisdom of my Brother Wendall's dark and gloomy socio-economic forecast. I felt as though I might be sick if the evening didn't come to a close soon.

Also, the now familiar words like "the door to Long Beach" and other code phrases were being bantered about. I tried to remember exactly how many times I'd heard Brother Wendall use these exact same phrases and to whom.

"The days of the one man shows like the great Billy Graham crusades are over! Hundreds came to the Lord, but then they were left with nowhere to go and get discipled, causing them to fall by the wayside. God is moving in a new way now, through the homes and doors of towns across the land, revealing His plan of salvation through discipleship, so as not to get devoured by the wolves roaming about in hordes in sheep's clothing. Many of them are found right in the Pentecostal and charismatic movement!! God gave the Pentecostals tongues and they just ran wild with it. He gave the charismatics gifts of the Spirit and oh, don't get me even started on that! Why, Brother Bob once said that folks ought to be locked up for at least six months after they get the baptism in the Spirit!" He paused to hear expected laughter. "What the body of Christ needs now is discipline, Brother Gene!" Brother Wendall put his well-used fork down after finishing his second slice of pear pie. I wondered how on earth one man could consume so much food as greedily as any pig I'd ever seen.

My mind was a blur with the similar promises Brother Wendall had made in the not so distant past to others right here in my own hometown. Words almost identical had been pronounced to Sister Dolly and her family, their pastor, and even at Sister Parker's Bible study. How many others had been promised an equally illustrious position in the discipleship movement of the fellowship? My head was spinning with the possibilities and the meaning of just exactly what was happening right before my very eyes. Even more shocking was the fact that this "position" that was being dangled so temptingly in front of my father's face was apparently being given without the slightest concern for his walk with the Lord. To my knowledge, absolutely no profession of faith had been made and certainly no bona fide life changes had been exhibited up until this point. Could just *anyone* be offered the position of "the door" to their community by Brother Wendall? Or was this merely being offered as part of some sort of sales job by one of the greatest con artists I'd ever met?

As my mind swirled, Daddy and the guests had excused themselves from the table while the rest of us helped in the clean up of the meal. Without so much as an offer to bring a dish to the counter, Brother Wendall and the others followed my father who led them in a tour of his self-constructed shed and the tiny back yard where the pear and fig trees were planted. Our friendly dachshund weaved in out of the men's legs, obviously annoying Brother Wendall.

"C'mere girl. That's right. I gotcha." I cooed to Gee Gee as she softly licked my face. It was clear that my father's head was reeling with the possibilities of turning our back yard into some sort of latter day farm. I wasn't so sure how the neighbors would react to this adventure. It was after all, just a tiny back yard in a modest subdivision, not acreage in the country.

The idea of turning our home and yard in the little subdivision into a full-fledged farm had germinated in my father's mind. You could almost hear the ticking of his brain as we sat at the supper table the following evening. It was clear that a new scheme was being hatched within.

"Honey, I think we have no choice but to put in a wood stove in the corner of the living room, ya know?" Daddy said, his head bobbing up and down as we awaited my mother's meek approval.

"Well, ... I don't know." She answered unconvinced.

"Think of it. We would save on the gas bill! I could get all the wood we need and it could warm this house all through. You know when we were kids we had a wood stove and that was all we had. People have just gotten spoiled now is what. But with hard times a-comin', like Brother Wendall's been predicting, I think we best get on the ball! Oh, will you give me some more of them beans and rice, honey before you sit down." Daddy held out his plate to my mother who after serving everyone had yet to sit down and eat her own meal.

"Well, if you think it would save on the gas, then we might best look on into it, I suppose." Mama answered scraping the bottom of the pot for the last of the red beans.

"Yeah, we got plenty of room to add some chickens to the back yard, too. We use the droppings to mix in the dirt for the garden." He was thinking way ahead now. "We used to call that a compost pile."

"Ok, right, but now I can't eat. Could we please not discuss poop at the table?" Cathy frowned wiping her mouth with the napkin and pushing her plate to the side.

Before the week was out, the little shed was now filled with tiny, fluffy, yellow peeps, fifty roosters and fifty hens. My father, knowing far less about farming than he ever would admit to anyone, thought he had to have one rooster for each female. Our country born neighbors, the Prines, looked on in utter disbelief, and a bit of horror at the thought of living next door to a smelly chicken farm.

The days rushed by as the chickens grew at an alarming rate, quickly outgrowing their tiny incubators in the shed. The chickens had to be turned into the newly built pin in the back yard. My dad had constructed a nice sized one equipped with roosting houses for the night. He had always been creative in his construction skills.

"Gigi, Gigi, shut that barking up!" My mother yelled out the side door. "Good grief that dog is going to drive us all crazy!"

"Mama, first you put her out of the house, after she was used to being inside at night for four years. Now half her yard has been taken over by this huge chicken pin! What in the world do you expect her to do?" I asked.

"Well. I expect she'll get adjusted soon enough. At least I certainly hope so!" my mother said. "Maybe I will to." She added, surprisingly.

"Yeah, the brethern are going to be here Sunday with a tiller and we'll be tilling up the side yard for the garden. I'll have that fenced off where the dog can't get to it. She'll adjust eventually! Dogs get along with chickens in farms all the time!" My father endeavored to enlighten us.

"Oh brother." I sighed under my breath heading out the screen door with it smacking loudly behind me. I had shuffled my feet into the stiff shoes on the porch so quickly, the backs of them folded under my heels.

"C'mere Gigi. That's right, that's a good girl." I said to the tiny black and tan dog as she wriggled and rolled over, lapping up the rare attention. It seemed she had been completely tossed to the side by everyone. She was a smart dog and felt the changes keenly. It was clear just by the way she looked into my eyes as if to say "I'm trying to be a good girl. I don't know what everyone wants from me? Don't y'all love me anymore?" I tried to comfort her as best I could, talking gently to her and scratching her warm, soft ears.

Suddenly the little voice inside my head began to shout: 'There is no God! Brother Wendall is nothing but a lying hypocrite and you are a fool!' "I rebuke you Satan in the name of Jesus!" I mumbled back to the voice as I began a conversation with the evil inner voice. 'There is no heaven and no hell! You're just a simple-minded fool! Following others blindly, who brainwash you! The whole world can see it!' "No, no, I command you Satan to flee from me!" I repeated all the familiar commands and faith formulas I'd learned, although nothing seemed to work. The familiar gnawing fear that I'd completely lose my mind in the next second or two had swept over me, filling my thoughts till I could think of nothing else.

I noticed that my hands were trembling as I withdrew them from petting GiGi. The knowledge that these were completely irrational thoughts did nothing to bring comfort to my soul. I just *knew* I was going crazy and would end up in some state mental ward, tied up in a straight jacket! My heart pounded within my chest. I resolved that I might just speak to Mama and Daddy about it. Maybe they could help me.

That night after supper had been cleared away, Cathy had excused herself early to go to bed; something about a head cold or some such other malady. I couldn't concentrate long enough to remember. My opportunity arose when the TV had not yet been turned on for the evening.

"I have to tell y'all something." I said as I fingered the buttons on my shirt.

"What is it, Son?" Daddy asked, concerned.

"Well, I keep having these sort of, well, panic attacks or something. In my mind a voice will just pop out of nowhere and tell me things like, 'There is no God.' I rebuke Satan constantly, throughout the day and night, but nothing seems to work. I feel like he's trying to take over me and I'm going to go insane." I said nervously, wondering how they would respond to this. I could feel my mother's eyes boring into me like tiny laser beams.

"Have they been giving you some kind of drugs or something out there at that fellowship house?" My mother said as she craned her neck forward and squinted her eyes while she studied me up and down. I felt like a bug under a microscope. My heart sunk. This was a mistake! I could feel it. My mother did not understand what I had been trying to convey. "You know, Clarice told me . . ." Right then, she was cut off by my father.

"Honey will you please? That's not being helpful here." My Dad said, surprisingly coming to my rescue. "Dave, when I was a boy, I had similar times of being anxious about one thing or the other. I would get so involved in just one thing, I would get myself all in a state about it, worrying so much that I just couldn't think of anything else." Daddy's gentle tone was abruptly interrupted.

"But Gene, if he's under the attack of Satan . . ." My mother was cut off by my father's irritated tone.

"Just go into another room and leave me to talk with my son in private for awhile." My father said in a no nonsense tone. "Good grief, you're no help at all in times like these. You need to just listen."

Mama wandered into the kitchen, well within earshot of everything that was being said. She had the look of a person who was convinced in a matter, her resolve unmovable.

"You see Son, sometimes when a person tries to be too spiritual, they lose all sight of what God is really about. For instance, I can just walk outside and see a beautiful tree, the leaves blowing in the breeze, or smell a delicate flower and that brings God's presence to mind. So try not to think on such deep and heavy things all the time. Just relax, and enjoy the life God gave you. Do you see what I mean, Son?" Daddy looked at me in a knowing way that somehow brought comfort to me. I'd had no idea that he'd be the one to understand, at least partially.

"Yes sir." I responded, knowing in my heart that his words had the ring of the truth and beauty of God in them. However, as I rose to walk to my bedroom the nagging knowledge that Daddy was not even saved arose again, and stomped out the truth from my heart, like someone crushing a delicate flower beneath their feet. I'll call my buddy, Paul. Maybe he and Sister Dolly could offer some insight and help me on this.

Sunday came and Brother Wendall arrived with the promised tiller. Soon the lush green carpet of lovely sod was replaced by lumps of dirt, while our dog looked on with a sad expression, somehow knowing this was the end of her little world.

"Dave, we gotta pull that tree up to make room for the garden." Daddy said about the little magnolia tree I'd nursed from a sapling to its now six foot height. Her deep green leaves and beautiful fragrant white blooms had graced the supper table last summer as I proudly picked them for Mama. Seeing the look of dismay on my face, my father explained. "Now son, food's more important that flowers. You know you haven't been through hard times, but I'm telling you, when your belly hits your backbone with hunger, you don't care about flowers!"

But to my relief he agreed to transplant the tree to another spot in our back yard. I immediately began to dig around it in a way so as not to disturb the root system any more than was necessary.

"Ahh, I'd say it's time we rested our weary bones!" Brother Wendall called out from his perch in the folding chair. Somehow he seemed to spend most of the day settled there, while my mother waited on him hand and foot, bringing him snacks of cake and coffee, to tide him over until the big afternoon meal. His hands weren't even dirty and he didn't look like he'd broken a sweat.

"I need to inform you brethren that the Saturday night meetings at the fellowship house are going to be postponed while we get matters in order." Brother Wendall raised his eyebrows in a serious grimace. "But I am at liberty to tell you of a closed meeting that is to be held in Mobile and only the most mature and discipled believers are to be invited. The idea is for smaller groups of the 'babes in Christ' to take part in home gatherings. Only when they have proved themselves to be trustworthy in the deep matters of the Lord will they be asked to take part in these closed fellowships. Oh, the joy and depth of the learning that will take place at the disciple's feet!" Brother Wendall's words hung silently in the air as all looked on in open mouthed awe. Were *we* to be invited to these special meetings or did we still have to be proved before such an invitation would be extended.

Brother Wendall looked at each of us, one at a time before speaking. "Yes, it's time. You are all invited to this most special event." A small smile creased the corners of his mouth and his eyes twinkled as though he had just dropped a loaf of bread among the starving.

"Will the Saturday night meetings still take place?" I asked quietly, as sadness grew inside me.

Brother Wendall waited a moment before responding, carefully choosing his words as though to further tantalize the hungry little group which hung on his every syllable. "Well, Brother Dave, sometimes there will be and other times, as the Lord mandates, there won't. It's much more expedient that our brethren learn to grow in the Lord through discipleship and the deeper truths have to be taught behind closed doors sometimes." He said knowingly, as everyone nodded, seeming to understand and agree with him. I was confused. Perhaps the tension inside of me was causing me yet again, not to clearly understand the words the Lord wanted me to hear. Perhaps I really am losing my mind! I had to pull myself together and struggle with all my might for my mind to come under my control.

I rebuked Satan inside my head, knowing full well that he could hear me even though the words were not spoken!

"Brother Rollins will explain the details of this new revelation later as we are ready for it. You know babies have to first drink milk before they are ready for the meat of God's true word, or to understand the real meaning of discipleship! You know this great man of God has been attending our meetings lately and the Holy Spirit is showing him in abundant detail how we are to proceed and bring things into order." Brother Wendall spoke in hushed tones as though someone were listening who should not hear these words of wisdom.

I remembered the small framed man with the stern expression pasted across his thin lips, his brows furrowed as though someone had angered him. His back was straight as an arrow at all times, rigid, his hair cut to perfection, not a single strand out of place. An attractive younger, silent woman accompanied him and stayed within six feet of him wherever he went. Her long brown hair gently covered her slim shoulders. Her face was pretty, with large blue eyes and a meek expression shone through. She was held up to the women in our meetings as the spirit which they should all aspire to. Brother Rollins referred to her only as his 'hand maiden of the Lord.' I thought it odd that a married man would travel with a pretty young woman, 'hand maiden' or not. Still, no one questioned it, but rather accepted this behavior as though the Lord were showing us a new way in which to live.

He had spoken to the gathering after the last meeting at the House of Praise. "High praises should be the truest form of devotion to God. It's not a contest to see who can out sing the other! It's not a concert either! I'll be instructing you in the coming weeks on how your praises should be brought in line according to the scriptures. One more thing I'd like to point out and this is not for anyone's ears except yours! This is to be kept in the utmost confidence! There will be a private meeting of the true believers, God's disciples, in Mobil, AL in the coming weeks. Brother Wendall will let only the mature believers know of the exact date and location. There will be deep truths of the Lord revealed at this sacred event. The outside world is not to know about this. They couldn't possibly receive these truths, nor have they the ears to hear it. They would only hear it as the world hears and then the devil would pervert these precious revelations from God. You don't cast pearls before swine, as the scripture teaches us. If Brother Wendall chooses to include you, keep the information top secret!" The entire room at the fellowship was dead silent. Gone were the cheerful, happy go lucky expressions, brightened from praising and worshipping the Lord with joy and thanksgiving. Now somber faced, the people looked at no one and said nothing as they rose to leave the meeting.

My soul was overcome with deep sorrow. I wasn't completely sure why, but this only added to the weariness of my ever present fearfulness and anxiety attacks from Satan. I thought about calling my friend. Paul would lighten my spirit a bit and perhaps he could shed some light on his feelings about these desperately dismal "secret meetings". I hoped sincerely that that there was not something wrong with my spiritual perception.

"Hey man! What's happening, praise the Lord!" The cheerful voice sounded over the phone.

"Oh not too much, just fighting the devil as always." I said half-jokingly.

"Well tell that devil to just jump back into the pit he came from! What's going on anyway?" Paul asked.

"Oh, I guess I just kinda needed to talk to you about your take on the meetings lately, you know, the secrecy and the overall mood and spirit." I said, hoping sincerely that his answer would reflect the same thing my spirit was trying to tell me.

"Well, I guess the Lord will reveal himself in the secret meeting in Mobile, Dave." Paul responded, as though harboring some unknown revelation from me.

"Oh you're going to the meeting too?" I said, very relieved to know that my buddy would be there as well.

"Yeah, Brother Wendall stopped by our house on the way over to see you. He invited us to the special closed meeting and we're all anticipating much revelation and wisdom to come forth for those with ears to hear it." He answered.

"Uh huh. Well, I gotta go Paul. I think I'm supposed to be weeding the garden or something." I answered, ready to end the conversation.

"Ok, well, see you soon!" Paul responded.

"Yeah, bye" I was deeply disappointed that I would not be able to share my feelings with Paul, because I could tell he was very excited about the coming closed meeting. I guess it's best to just keep my feelings to myself for now, I concluded.

The weeks leading up to the meeting were some of the worst I'd ever experienced. The headaches and fearfulness intensified in both severity and length. Mama made an appointment for me at the local doctor's office where I received a prescription for a mild sedative. The prescription had a calming effect that did help my physical sense of well-being, but guilt soon swept over me like a tide in a hurricane, making me feel as though I had failed to have enough faith in God to heal and deliver me, so I soon quit the prescription. The headaches and attacks from Satan returned with an even stronger vengeance than before. Maybe Paul was right. Maybe the "secret meetings" would bring forth the Lord's wisdom which would have a healing effect on me. I had finally begun to respond somewhat differently to all those who asked how I was doing. "I have gotten the victory"! This seemed to more than satisfy most folks and they would offer no further inquiry.

The day of the meeting arrived with much excitement. It turned out not to be very "secret" after all because it seemed that nearly everyone associated with the House of Praise was in attendance. Paul, Cathy, Cindy and I all rode in the van from the fellowship along with some others. Our parents followed behind in separate cars. I wanted to feel the same excitement displayed by others, but somehow it just wasn't there.

"I've such a deep revelation from the Lord" Cindy piped up with a glazed look in her eyes.

"Well share that with us, Cindy!" Paul added smiling.

"Well, the Lord showed me that we, all of us here, and everyone there in Mobile . . . . we are all coming together for just *one* purpose!" Cindy said smiling, near tears.

"Wow, bless God!" Paul added, apparently understanding this 'word from the Lord' far more than I did.

From the corner of my eyes I could see Cathy nodding her head in agreement. They *all* were able to comprehend the deeper meaning behind this revelation, all except for me. I seemed to be the odd man out and my apprehension only swelled at this latest "truth" from God.

The ride to Mobile seemed never-ending. Finally we reached the large motel in the downtown area of Mobile, close to the waterfront where the view of Mobile Bay with the ships coming in to port was visible. The town looked large in comparison to Long Beach, its buildings towering up to levels I'd never seen. The motel must have had ten floors! A skyscraper! The old historic buildings reminded me of antebellum ladies from the old south, their glory days behind them, but still the beauty of the structures were a treat to the eyes.

The scenic view of Mobile that had so briefly lifted my spirits was quickly squelched as we entered the austere, somber atmosphere of the "special meeting." Our group quietly seated itself, without having spoken a word to anyone, nor anyone speaking a word to us. The effort at appearing to be dignified and submitted fell flat, seeming more like an act. I shivered, with an icy coldness throughout my body. I recalled a similar feeling from my past experience. But when was it? Oh yes, now I remember! Once when my brother Ronnie had been drafted, we went to visit him at boot camp on Paris Island during the height of the Vietnam War. The atmosphere among the rank and file felt much the same as this, yet not quite as grave.

"Uh um! We will come to order and sing a hymn of praise to the Lord. All rise." The stern looking man with salt and pepper hair and an ill-fitting, out of date suit demanded.

The lady playing the piano quietly played the chorus watching the man at the podium for cues as though he were an orchestral director. I watched as the group of people unknown to us all at once raised their arms at shoulder height, again, being directed by the man at the podium. Suddenly, everyone stopped and silence filled the air. The second and then third chorus took place, much the same as the first. At the end of the third song, all were simultaneously directed to sing high praises. The pianist played a few simple chords first up and then down the keyboard, with the sustain pedal to the floor, bumping the crowd from one note to the next.

I dared to peek from the corner of my eyes seeing more than half the crowd simply standing, rigidly, as though perhaps bored with the entire effort of singing praises as a body of believers.

Just as abruptly as it had begun, the singing and playing stopped, whereupon a booming male voice could be heard as he began to prophecy:

"Hear my voice, all ye people of the lands! I am bringing forth an army from the East and an army from the West. I am gathering first one utensil and then another, from the ends of the earth, which will usher in my kingdom, saith the Lord God!"

Silence once again filled the air. Yet another man took the podium. At this point, they all seemed to look the same. Perhaps the similarity was in the tone of their voice, or the rigidness of their backs, or just the overall sense of austere sternness which emanated from their countenance.

"There are costs which much be covered by the flock. Just as the sheep of the flock must be shorn for their wool to provide for the benefit of the shepherd, so must the flock of the Lord bring forth their efforts and gifts to God's work. This is the time." This was all that was spoken before several men acting as ushers, began to pass simple baskets from row to row, each person making a bit too much of a show of reaching into bill folds and seemingly emptying them out for the Lord.

As soon as the collection had been taken, the long anticipated moment had arrived! It was time for the very first new revelation to be opened up to God's people. I could hardly wait to hear what the Lord so wanted to reveal in secret to his most beloved believers, the anointed ones who were to usher in His second coming and change this world forever!

The man, unannounced, approached the podium. The rustle of his suit could be heard due to the silence in the crowd. No one moved a muscle as all eyes were focused forward. Not even a hint of a smile would crease his thin lips. His long nose added to his grim appearance. Dark hair piled at least two inches high on top of his head, neatly and firmly slicked back and held in place with obviously copious amounts of hair oil.

"Praise be to God." The monotone voice said as the crowd responded in kind.

"We are all here to learn tonight . . . . to learn how to worship properly, in order and with respect as is good and pleasing in the sight of the Lord. We are not to act as sheep without a shepherd! No! We have shepherds, and the sheep should listen and obey the shepherds of the Lord! Disobedience is an abomination before God and will not be tolerated! Discipleship in its truest form is complete and total submission to your shepherd and therefore to God. For our married women, this means complete obedience and submission to your husbands, since they have authority over you. You are to obey his commands as though the Lord were giving them. This is just and pleasing before God. So for wives, your coverings are to be your husbands. Husbands, you are to submit to your shepherds." His words droned on and on and repeated with all the repetition of a drum beat, and were now blending together in one monotonous message.

At long last, as the crowd began to shift uncomfortably in their seats, the meeting was dismissed as abruptly as it began. Everyone filed out to their respective cars to leave, almost without words, as though trying to impress the hierarchy with their silent submission, their stances reflecting the stiff backed leaders.

The mood on the trip home was quite different than our ride over here. Gone was the undertone of excitement at hearing the message from the Lord. Now our emotions reflected the service and the trip home was spent in near silence.

The following day at dinner, my mother broke the ice while serving us our meal.

"Well that was just about the coldest bunch of folks I ever came across in all my born days!" She exclaimed as she plopped a scoop of mashed potatoes onto Daddy's plate.

"Yeah, remind me not to go to the next closed meeting! I'm not interested in any more of that!" Cathy chimed in. "Pass the pepper will you please?"

"Well I'm relieved that's out in the open!" Daddy said echoing my sentiments exactly.

"At least we still have the Saturday night meetings at the House of Praise! Well that is if they ever start having them again." I offered.

Later that day, Brother Wendall called to invite us to a workday at the fellowship house, which was to be followed by a meal. The Saturday night following the day of work, a believer's meeting was scheduled to be held. I could only hope to hang on until that time when surely brighter days were to come! Only a few more weeks now, and we could actually have some real high praises again, just like in days gone by.

CHAPTER 7

THE EXIT

To everything there is a season
And a time to every purpose under the heaven (Ecclesiastes 3:1)

A warm spring breeze played across my arm which was positioned on the car door as we pulled into the driveway of the fellowship house for the workday. The sun shone brightly, warming the air which was perfumed by the honeysuckle vine that grew wild through the camellia bush by the house. Even the birds seemed to be enjoying this day as they sang their songs for the gathering crowd of people who had arrived ready to help Brother Wendall in the clean up effort.

"Gigi, don't run off girl. Come back here." I called out to our soon to be ex-pet. Daddy was already taking long, brisk strides toward Brother

Douglas who had agreed to take her as his own dog. "There's a good girl." I said sadly as I watched her shiny black tail wagging quickly as she romped through the bright green, long grass, completely unaware that her life was about to change with the inevitable loss of her people. I swallowed back the lump that now formed in my throat.

"Well Brother Dave, let's see if this bottle of window cleaner will fit your hands" sister Dolly said happily as she thrust the bottle into one of my hands and the paper towels into the other. I could see my dad scooping up Gigi and walking away with her. This morning was probably the last time I'd ever see her or pet her soft coat. "Why yes indeed it does! You can get started on the exterior of all these windows." I had just been assigned the odious task of scrubbing windows so filthy you could barely see through to the other side. One little bottle of blue cleaner hardly seemed ample for the grueling task before me. "Don't worry Dave, they won't bite." Sister Dolly said as she chuckled walking past me and back inside.

"Hey Brother Dave, you got the *cool* job! I'm so jealous!" Dean walked by, slapping me on the back. I could hear his tool belt busily jingling as he passed me, apparently off to some more important task.

"Yeah, I'm just lucky I suppose." I said, trying to force a smile. Still, it was nice to see my friends. Some of them even greeted me with a hug, as was still the custom among the "less mature" and younger believers.

The morning droned by, with only the sound of Deans's tool belt as he continued making his way to first one work project and then another, never really getting involved with much of anything and accomplishing nothing, other than the exercise of walking. Still, the jingling did break the monotony of scrubbing years of filth off the dirt-caked panes of glass as well as giving Dean the appearance of being busy about important jobs.

At long last, sister Dolly came out and called everyone in for a lunch break, which consisted of sandwiches and iced tea. After quickly inhaling my sandwich and draining the last drop of good ole' southern sweet tea, I made my way into the kitchen for a refill. Brother Ron and Brother Andy were leaning against the kitchen counter with their backs toward me, as I quietly walked in and overheard them chuckling.

"Mmm, yeah, wouldn't she make just the best little concubine you could ever want?" Brother Andy said while looking out the kitchen door.

"Don't you just know it brother? We'd have to do some sharing with her." Brother Ron said, craning his neck for a better look.

I glanced out the door and to my great surprise I saw my sister, Cathy standing on the stoop, shaking rugs. Overhearing the conversation, she turned and scowled in their direction.

"Ok, so what does 'concubine' mean anyway? I've never heard of that one." Cathy said, trying not to sound too immature.

"Oh you're such a baby in the Lord." Brother Ron said laughing.

"I'm *not* a baby!" My sister said, her pride hurt and obviously embarrassed by the tone of the conversation. I quickly grabbed my sandwich and another glass of tea and made a fast exit from the room.

Although not yet well versed enough in King James English to have understood the meaning of the word concubine, I was given the distinct impression that she had just been either insulted or possibly even complimented in an inappropriate manner. These remarks were not the first suggestive ones I'd heard from these two brothers in recent weeks. Off color humor was gradually becoming commonplace here at the House of Praise.

My mind left the current portrait of what the fellowship had become and drifted to the joyful time when glorious meetings took place and beautiful, euphoric high praises rang throughout the house. Conversations back in those days were not peppered with indecent innuendos, but rather salted with the love of God and one another.

Leaving for home after a long hard work day, my eyes fell upon the now faded sign that read "The House of Praise . . . Where Jesus is Lord!" Brother Wendall had recently said: "This isn't just simply the House of Praise anymore! This is my home! That sign is really out dated you know. We've grown past the need for such worldly displays. Or at least we *should* have!" His brown eyes darted and pierced through each of us, daring anyone to object. I felt as though I was losing my grasp on the very heart of all that was happiness, all that was joy and the very presence of God. Everything seemed to be changing so fast. Could it be that I was just not maturing in the Lord as the others were? I couldn't bear the thought of not feeling the presence of the Lord and the fellowship of the people of God. This place was the life preserver to which I clung! Another memory drifted by like a cloud inside my mind.

"I'm being stationed to Texas, you know? I'm leaving out the middle of this very week." Dean had said holding a half-eaten sandwich in his hand.

"Oh, . . . well, how long you gonna be there?" I asked, saddened that my good friend was leaving.

"Well, you know I'm signed up for a three-year stint. They call the shots, so I will probably never be back at Keesler." Dean said taking another bite of the sandwich.

"I'll miss you, yank." I said to him, fighting the lump forming in my throat. "You know anyone born north of Jackson, Mississippi qualifies as a sure enough Yankee! But I forgive you for it. It's not your fault." I said to lighten the mood.

'Yeah right, Dave. You're so well traveled and broad-minded. Just the kind of guy I like to hang around with!" He laughed. "Hey why don't you make use of yourself and grab the other end of this ladder, alright?" Dean said smiling as he snatched up one end of the beat up old ladder. "The bulbs in the chandeliers of this old farm house are hard to change with the ceilings being so high up. They not that high where I come from."

"Again, that's because you're a Yankee-man!" I said laughing and picking up the other end of the battered ladder. "The ceilings were all built high in these old houses because there was no air-conditioning back when they were built. On a hot summer's day, the heat would rise up and then you would open the transoms with a hook attached to a long stick. That would let the hot air escape, while the over-sized windows let in the fresh, somewhat cooler air."

"Well then you live and you learn, eh sport? The south sure is full of some different cultures though. You almost need a passport to come down here!" Dean said climbing up the high ladder.

"Yeah, I guess. Things seem really different to me when I visit my relatives up north." I said fumbling for words. The question that burned in my brain had to come out. "Uh, hey Dean, you stay out here on weekends sometimes and know the inside scoop on just about everyone around I guess." I said quietly. "Ohm, well, has brother Wendall ever asked you to do anything kind of, well, ohm, strange? You know what I mean?"

"Hmm, let me think about it for a minute. Strange, you mean weird stuff like insisting I put some sauerkraut on my hotdog?" Dennis said laughing innocently. His schoolboy face had the appearance of a young shepherd that might be tending a flock in some far away land, scrubbed in sunshine and naïve in the ways of the outside world.

"No no, I mean, well, err, you know, kind of things he might ask of you, well, at night, kind of weird stuff." I felt the heat burning from my neck up to my face and knew that I was surely blushing. I looked down at the worn carpet to hide my face.

Apparently he had been spared the grotesque advances of the head Shepherd of the fellowship. My mind had retreated into sort of a fog ever since that night and I had to admit that I had begun to doubt myself on the accuracy of exactly what really took place. The need for increased amounts of sleep and a feeling of constant exhaustion had now replaced the panic attacks which had been overwhelming. But these days, even the simplest of tasks required more concentration than I was able to muster at times. Could I have somehow twisted everything up and distorted the nature of Brother Wendell's actions? I doubted my own sanity at times, and perhaps this whole memory had become somewhat distorted by now.

"Dave, hey man, you ok? I mean is something bothering you that I can pray with you about or anything?" Dean asked as he came down from the ladder, apparently noticing the troubled look about my face. I had to pull myself together so he couldn't see that I was under the attack of Satan! I didn't want anyone to know the truth, whatever it was!

"Dave, you and Cathy need to help me clean up behind the chickens and feed them as soon as we get home." Daddy stated.

My mind snapped back from the memories of the day, only to catch a glimpse of my beloved dog Gigi, now following closely behind her new master's heels. "Please God, let him take good care of my dog and let her not miss us too much." I prayed inside my mind.

"Cathy you're mighty quiet today. I guess you're kind of tired from the work, huh?" My father asked my sister, who was silently staring out of the window.

"What?" Cathy turned her head around to face Daddy, her long hair blowing in the wind. I could see streaks down her cheeks. Had she been crying?

"Where in the world is your mind?" Daddy remarked. "Sometimes I wonder what's becoming of this family nowadays! Everyone seems to be in a daze all the time."

"Well, Gene, maybe the kids are just tired out a little from workin' all day out here." My mother said in an attempt to keep the peace.

That week Cathy would be turning fifteen. I couldn't help but notice as she stood in the kitchen drying dishes from the cake she and Mama had just baked, that she looked sad. She went about her chores quietly, unlike the old chatterbox who was usually either talking or singing. The silence was broken when Paul drove up in his mother's station wagon. The wood panels gleamed in the sun on this beautiful spring day.

"Come on in Paul, after you take your shoes off." Mama instructed.

"Oh yes m'am." Paul replied already taking them off while his guitar was still slung around his neck.

"Here comes Cindy and Karla too." Paul said coming inside, the screen door smacking behind him.

"Oh Cindy, Karla, y'all came! I'm so glad!" Cathy said, her countenance brightening up at their appearance. "Hey Paul, I'm glad you brought your guitar. Maybe you can serenade me." Cathy teased with a wink. She and Paul had been nothing more than chums, and always enjoyed kidding around with one another.

"Hey Mrs. Woods, hey Paul." Cindy drawled as she nearly cooed when seeing Paul. It was obvious to all that she had a huge crush on him, all except Paul that is. He was completely oblivious.

"We brought something for the birthday girl." Cindy said as Karla appeared in the kitchen smiling, holding a brightly colored package with a huge shiny golden bow on top of it.

"Oh now I said no one had to bring a gift! I only wanted you to come over and spend a little time with me! That's gift enough! How pretty the wrapping is! It's almost too pretty to open!" Cathy said excitedly as she began to carefully un-wrap the parcel.

Cindy and Karla could not contain their snickers. Apparently they were up to some mischief and it was probably going to be aimed at Cathy's expense.

The "gift" when opened contained a few ears of some very oddly colored corn. I remembered seeing it at the A & P and it was called Indian corn. It was a seasonal item, available in the fall. Apparently some people bought it to make table arrangements. This corn they presented her with was obviously old, the leaves withered and dried.

"Oh it's just beautiful. Look everyone, my favorite colors too! How thoughtful of you." Cathy said with genuine appreciation in both her face and her voice.

Apparently her sincere appreciation for this cruel hoax somehow took the wind right out of Cindy and Karla's sails as their expression turned from mischievous grins to aggravated frowns. "Cathy . . . . it's a *joke!*" Cindy cackled. "Good grief, don't you even know what Indian corn is?"

"Well no I don't, but it's really pretty and I'll put it on my dresser to decorate my room. Cathy said embarrassed.

I could see tears welling up in her eyes as she realized she was meant to be the brunt of a joke, and on her birthday at that, by the very girls she so wanted to befriend her. Paul must have noticed, too as he swung his guitar around. "Hey it's time to sing for the birthday girl! Happy Birthday to you, happy birthday to you, happy birthday dear Cathy, happy birthday to you!" Paul sang, bringing a smile to her face.

"Ok let's cut the cake." Cathy said ready to enjoy what was left of the small celebration.

I was relieved I wasn't asked to play the piano. I knew I could not hold my concentration even long enough for this simple tune. I had not pursued any lessons and playing "in the spirit" was not going well at all. Discouraged, I had allowed the piano to gather dust in the corner of the living room.

"Hey did y'all see Carson last night?" Cindy piped up looking knowingly at Karla who started to chuckle with her hand over her mouth as though it was something wicked with which they both shared this spicy secret.

"No, we don't watch that." Cathy said with a puzzled look on her face. Our own family had stopped watching that show quite some time back due to the sometimes gutter humor that had become more frequent as time went by and censor controls were loosened.

In previous months at the fellowship house, television had been completely taboo! No one trying to live in the spirit would have dared watch too much, if any television, much less, late night television! However, recently I noticed that Brother Wendall had purchased a TV for their living room, saying he needed to "keep up with current events." He had also stated he needed to establish "common ground" in order to bring more sheep into the fold. But with the recent crudeness being displayed by the supposedly "more mature" Christians at the House of Praise, I had to wonder just how much more common our ground had to become before the line between the world and us became indistinguishable.

At last the night of the "open believers" meeting had arrived. I couldn't help but notice as I parked my car, that there were very few others. In times past, finding a place to park was difficult, with vehicles piled up like sardines in a can. But now everything seemed to be changing. Five long weeks had gone by since the last meeting and my spirit was parched like a wilting flower in a desert, very much in need of the Holy Spirit to rain down His presence!

"Good evening Brother Dave." A very solemn looking brother Wendall greeted me at the door, wearing an ill-fitting suit. He'd put on quite a bit of weight in recent weeks and the buttons were about to pop on his sport coat.

"Well you're dressed up. As a matter of fact, so is everyone, except for me that is." I said feeling the heat of embarrassment rising to my face.

"Well Dave, we've been following the lead of Brother Rollins and taking his advice to heart", Brother Wendall solemnly reminded me.

"Oh, yeah, right." I said fumbling for an explanation for my casual blue jeans and loose hanging shirt. As I looked around the room, gone were the flannel shirt and blue jean clad men, shouting joyfully: "Praise the Lord!" Also missing were the quaint looking maxi skirts and long flowing hair of most of the young ladies. The entire atmosphere now resembled more of a stiff business meeting rather than the warm and inviting fellowship meetings of the past.

The chairs were lined up neatly in rows on the worn rug where once we all sat on throw pillows or just Indian style on the floor. Two young attractive girls were motioned to the front by Brother Rollins, his newest handmaidens. With a tug of their mini-skirts, they swayed their hips seductively and took their places beside him to assist in the leading of the singing and worship, so as to keep the rest of us "in line and order" as brother Wendall had been repeating ad nauseum. "You have many people who would be rebellious and go out on their own during the worship service," he had said.

"Brethren, it's time that we all come to order in service of the Lord" brother Rollins' voice rang out as he rubbed his hands together standing at the front of the room. I couldn't help but notice the lovesick expressions on the faces of his two "hand-maidens" as they gazed admiringly at him. The light from the old chandelier above that had just been cleaned was brighter now with all the bulbs replaced and the crystals sparkling, reflecting the light which caught a shimmer of gold on Brother Rollins' left hand. His wedding ring glistened and glimmered. "I think it would be in order if we taught you a new chorus to sing. Please allow the Lord to lead you as you sing along" he said, indicating that his handmaidens should now join him in leading the new song. "Thou hast shown thee oh man what is good, and what doth the Lord require of thee, but to do justly and to love mercy and to walk humbly with thy God."

The song was easy to sing, with a simple melody that anyone could follow. The faces around the room looked somewhat grim as they worshipped the Lord, though. The smiles and laughter of days gone by, now seemed just a memory, tucked away in the corner of my mind. The once familiar high praises, were stifled as the believers looked to Brother Rollins for permission before attempting that level of worship. As he lifted his hand indicating authorization was given, some of the women and men attempted to sing in the spirit, but their efforts fell flat. Brother Rollins stood erect looking on, his lips in a firm grimace as though the sound which fell on his ears was painful to endure.

"Brethren and Sisters of the Lord, he has shown me new revelations and knowledge in the spirit this week and has directed that I should share this with you. Those who have ears ought to hear! This is the word of the Lord!" Brother Rollins moved his hand upward and then smoothed his blond hair which seemed to be all in one piece, not a single hair out of place. I tried listening to his "revelations" but my mind wandered as he droned on and on repeating the same phrases in a monotonous cacophony. I couldn't help but notice the fidgeting going on in the room by nearly everyone as the series of revelations finally came to an end.

"Brother Rollins, I wonder could you pray for me?" Sister Price raised her hand in the back of the room. "I had been healed, but the swelling in my hands has returned, see?" The twisting of her swollen fingers was obviously rheumatoid arthritis in a severe stage.

"Sister, I have the anointing oil right here" brother Wendall said automatically coming to her aid while the entire crowd of believers outstretched sympathetic hands toward a much loved member of the body of Christ. Tears flowed from Sister Price's aged and care worn eyes as she received a much needed outpouring of love and support from her friends.

"Thank you. God bless you, each and every one." She said gratefully.

For a brief moment, the tender hearted caring that I remembered from this group of people came to the surface, flickered brightly, then died away once more as Brother Rollins stepped in.

"Ok members, from now on, we will have a certain time set up so that these requests can be handled in order." He said loudly, quieting the entire crowd who looked like recalcitrant children, feeling guilty for moving "out of order".

Everyone in the room looked at one another feeling the sting of being chastised by their lofty new shepherd. "I think we should all take this wisdom with us on our journey home this evening. The body of Christ will gather again soon. I'll be in touch to let you know when that will be." Brother Wendall announced.

The crowd began to disburse quietly and quickly, without our usual closing prayer. "Hey spiffy tie, Brother Larry. You look quite the sport tonight there man!" Paul teased Larry as he flipped his tie loose from his sport coat.

"I know, but brother Wendall made us all dress up tonight." Larry replied as he uncomfortably straightened his neck tie.

"Well I think he looks handsome." Cathy added emphatically. "Besides Paul, you could take a lesson. You know plaid pants really shouldn't be worn with that tie-dyed t-shirt,." Cathy laughed, punching Paul.

"Why you squirt, I oughtta . . ." Paul said laughing. "Hey y'all, I think maybe we should head on over to the pizza place." I added quietly. "We have some folks staring at us." I had suddenly noticed that we were the only guests still standing in the front room.

"Oh yeah right, well, let's cruise on over there then. I missed lunch today anyway, fasting you know." Paul said.

"Fasting? I thought I saw you polishing off an ice cream after school today?" Cathy asked.

"Well, you'll learn as you grow in the Lord that there are many kinds of fasts, Cathy. Today, I was only fasting from full meals." Paul said seriously.

"Really? You mean you can eat ice cream and still be fasting?" Cathy asked.

"Well, sometimes. It all depends on the type of fast that the Lord has led you to go on." Paul answered.

"I sure wish I'd known this a long time ago." Cathy added.

"Well there are a lot of things a younger Christian hasn't learned yet." Paul added, being the mature one.

The following Sunday came quickly and I could hear Mama as the pots and pans clattered in the kitchen, water running and glasses being filled with ice as Mama struggled to get supper ready by 5:00 on the dot.

"Y'all c'mon now . . . . get in here before it gets cold." I heard the usual supper time summons.

"You don't have to call me twice! Sure smells good my lady!" Daddy said as he swooped into his chair like a hawk settling in with a delectable bite of prey about to be clutched tightly in his claws.

"Well here ya go Gene." Mama said, giving Daddy a large scoop of the dark brown stew filled with beef, potatoes and carrots. "Good nourishing meal there for ya . . . and cheap too!" Mama said boasting.

"That's the best kind Mama! Gotta watch what we spend, especially these days." Daddy said bobbing his head up and down in agreement with himself.

Cathy and I looked at one another and rolled our eyes simultaneously, hoping we were not in for yet another sermon on the coming 'hard times'.

"Well now I just have to say it, and ain't no other way of putting it but to just tell what's the God's honest truth of it." Mama said finally sitting down after serving each of us and then herself last.

"That was just about the most boring meeting we ever went to last night! Wasn't nothing like church a'tall!" Mama said shaking her head. "And did you see them gals of that man, Mr. Rollins? What did he call 'em 'handmadens' or some such a nonsense? Why they had them skirts a' hiked up sky high is what! Now I don't care what he calls 'em, but Christian girls ain't got no call to go prissin' all about like some kind a street walker! No sir!" Mama looked to Daddy for confirmation.

"I'll have to admit, they sure did have a hitch in their get-a-long's!" Daddy said laughing. "And it was all I could do to keep from yawning while Brother Rollins repeated his words over and over again. I thought I'd get sea sick with the motions of his hands to emphasize 'brethren, behold, the Lord reveals his truths through his witness this night in your face!' I thought if only I didn't have to see *his* face smirking I might be able to get through the night without going to sleep!" Daddy said with a final slurp of his stew. "Gimme another bowl of that there stew, huh Mama." He requested as Mama was already half way to the stove to refill his empty bowl.

"Oh and I didn't dare raise my hands to praise the Lord! I didn't want to feel the icy glare from those cold eyes of that Brother Rollins feller! And ain't he the one with those beady little fish eyes? I never did trust a man with cold eyes and I'm tellin' you the gospel truth, so help me but that man has got 'em!" Mama declared in her usual southern drawl.

Cathy erupted with laughter at this point and everyone turned to her. "I'm sorry, but I just can't help it. I felt about a hundred pounds of pressure on me when I was there. I surely could never measure up to the women folks of the House of Praise and felt like they just wanted me to sit in the corner like some insignificant little imp that wasn't worthy to be in their presence or breathe the same air as the high and mighty 'brother Rollins'!" Cathy stated.

"Huh! He ain't so high and mighty as he thinks. He's in for a come-up-ence if you asked me!" Mama said looking around the small wooden dinner table and then casting her glance at me for approval. "What do you think about all this Dave?"

Suddenly all eyes were upon me, awaiting my opinion. I felt a flood of emotions rushing through me such as fear, sadness, and yes, relief. The 'House of Praise' and the services held there had become much more to me than even my own family members. It was my life being, my reason for living, and my entire belief system. Ever since 'the incident' though, my foundation had somewhat of a crack in it. That crack was now widening as the entire house of cards was about to crumble.

"Well, I think, that is I mean to say, well, I did feel a heaviness, an oppression throughout the service, but then I thought that it was probably just me, because, well, I feel that way a lot, you know?" I quickly cast my eyes downward looking at my still full bowl of stew. I'd only picked at the contents while listening to my family talking about the things that had already swirled in my brain. But yet, I'd struggled to push these thoughts away from me, thinking that surely Satan was whispering more foolish ideas in my head.

"No Dave, it wasn't you! It's *them*!" Mama repeated.

"That's right son. I've been seeing it you, know, but I figured I'd let you all come to that on your own." Daddy said with his chest sticking out in pride at his revelation. "You know your old Daddy does see these things." He said with a final slurp, finishing his second bowl of stew. However there was a reluctance as of yet to completely agree with the way that the rest of us were obviously feeling. Certainly the pecking order in this shepherding or discipleship movement favored 'the man of the house' above all, so perhaps he had not felt the full burden of the bonds that were choking the rest of us.

"Well I know that I feared to sing out to the Lord at all. Y'all know how I love to sing to God and I promise I'm not doing it to call attention to myself! But I'm telling you, I just felt it was best to sing quietly and stay in the same monotone key as everyone else rather than get that 'you're out of order there, sister' look from that man again!" Cathy said with tears stinging her eyes. I never realized she felt this way and it obviously hurt her to the core to be forced to behave in a way she was not created for, like a square peg trying to squeeze into a round hole. Why couldn't we all just be accepted for who we were and appreciated for the way God had made us?

"And the way those men have been eyeing me lately, just makes my skin crawl Daddy." She said looking at him pleadingly.

At that moment, I saw something completely snap the ties that bound my father to the House of Praise. Obviously, he had gotten the full meaning of the message my sister was trying to convey.

"I think it's time we cut the ties with that place before we get in any deeper. We need to submit to the Lord and not to any man. I've had enough of this and I say it's over as of this minute!" Daddy smacked his hand on the table in righteous indignation.

"I think you're right." Mama said agreeing with Daddy.

They looked in my direction and I shook my head and muttered, "Yes, mm hum." Shaking my head in full agreement I felt the weight of the world lift from my shoulders. My dad was right. Now our family was, for probably the first time, in complete harmony and knowing that we must take the first step out of the muck and mire of the so called 'House of Praise'. It felt as though we were leaving a brick making pit in which we had been marching around in the mud, trying to make bricks with no straw, like the Israelites in the old movie I'd seen on television.

"Now I still believe that we need to be Spirit-filled and I don't want to go back to our old church." I added fearing that we would have to go back to something which I felt would not feed my soul.

"Oh Gene, now I just don't think I can take going back to St. Thomas!" Mama added. She had never been a staunch Catholic and had secretly always wanted to break with that church.

"Nope, we're a family and we'll just have church right here once a week and read God's Word and learn as a family . . . together." Daddy answered.

I noticed Cathy wiping a tear from her cheek. This supper had turned into quite the event, completely unplanned, unrehearsed, and entirely necessary.

"Gene are we gonna call 'em or anything?" Mama looked at Daddy questioningly.

"If there's any calling to be done, I'll be the one doing it!" My father said as he pointed his thumb rigidly into his chest.

Deep down, I wondered just how this 'family church' thing was going to work. However, the feeling of release from the inhumane bondage that these men had been placing on the backs of all who wished to serve the Lord at the House of Praise, by far outweighed any concerns I may have over family Bible studies. I could deal with 'home church' far easier. How had this road to follow the Lord ended up this way? How had I gone so wrong, when it all *felt* so right?

The sound of Cathy weeping brought me out of my reverie. She had quietly excused herself and was now in the privacy of her tiny room. I had no doubt she was feeling a similar sense of both release and sorrow as I was.

"Mama, I'll be back later." I said as I grabbed my car keys and began to walk out of the kitchen.

"Where ya goin' off to Dave?" She asked.

"Oh just for a drive. I'll be back later." I said shoving my feet into the worn, but comfortable sneakers that sat in a line of other shoes on the porch floor.

"Ok, well be careful then son." Mama said, as she began to clatter the dishes into the small, metal sink.

The evening air was cool and felt refreshing as it blew across my face. The scent of the salty sea revived my senses as I drove down the highway. The screeching of the gulls following the shrimp boats that came in for the evening was a comforting sound, one I had grown up with. Parking my car in a narrow spot, I decided to go for a short walk and enjoy the day's end watching the sun set across the Gulf of Mexico. The seas seemed to calm down with the setting sun which cast glorious, brilliant colors of pinks and purple across the horizon.

"Lord, I don't know how this all happened, but I know I still love you . . . no matter what and I want to follow you! Lord, lead me and guide me. I don't know what to do or where to go. So I come to you. My Jesus, I trust in you!"

The top of the sun finally sank into the ocean's depths and the cries of the gulls were replaced with nothing but the sounds of the waves. Breathing in the salty air deeply into my lungs, I walked back to my car. "I think I need to talk to my buddy Paul about this whole thing".

As I walked up the familiar driveway, it now seemed a bit foreign to me. I had something to say to Paul and wasn't exactly sure how it would be received. I'd hoped that this situation would not hinder our friendship, but there was no getting around the fact that I would no longer be involved in any way shape or form with the place which had become our haven. Our entire friendship had revolved around the weekly services and fellowship up until today.

"Well, well Brother David, it's always a pleasure to see you. Paul's back in his room playing the guitar. Go on back. I know he'll be pleased to see you!" Sister Dolly said cheerfully as she swept a strand of red hair back up into the beehive hairdo, a dishtowel thrown across her shoulder. "I just have to get these supper dishes finished."

"Hey man, good to see ya! What's goin' on?" Paul said smiling up at me from behind the well worn acoustic guitar that he strummed, its gentle tunes soothing my jangled nerves.

"Quite a lot, actually. I uh, well, I just came over here to talk to you about it all." I said nervously. The small room was close to the kitchen, and I heard the clattering of dish washing come to a sudden halt.

I tried to choose my words wisely, but felt myself jumping headlong into the heart of the matter as though I could no longer hold in the secret. "My family has decided we aren't going to go back to the House of Praise anymore." I said quickly.

Paul's eyes flew open as did his mouth upon hearing my statement. Then as I continued, he furrowed his brow together as though weighing each word I said with a certain amount of disdain. Sister Dolly had now completely left her kitchen task and stood at the door of Paul's room as we continued the conversation. "When did this big decision take place Dave?" Paul asked setting down his guitar on the bunk bed beside him.

"It was just at supper time today. Somehow it all just sort of came out. We had all been feeling the same things, but had kept it to ourselves until someone mentioned, I'm not even sure who, that the recent meetings were awfully oppressive. Then it all spilled out. We were sick of hearing about 'discipleship this and submission that'. It was just all more than we could take. Before we knew it, everyone just felt such a big release and the decision was made that it would be best if we broke ties and had done with it all at once." I ended as the words had just poured out of me. It felt better to now have the truth out in the open. I had done it!

"Well Dave, I think you had best be very careful." Sister Dolly said with a concerned look upon her face. "You will all be out from the covering of your shepherd and a strong fellowship of believers. I mean you will be open to every attack that Satan has! I'm not trying to scare you, but you really should pray about this some more. We need the protection of our shepherds!" Sister Dolly warned.

"But that's it in a nutshell . . . . the Bible says 'the Lord is my shepherd, I shall not want.' I don't think it's any of the Lord's doing to have us all so heavily yoked in such bondage like some sort of ox out in the fields. I'm not an ox. I'm a child of God and from now on that's just exactly who I will be following, not some man who wants to put himself in the seat of the Lord." My own words and the boldness of them, although spoken with a tone of respect, shocked me. Right at that moment, the full brunt of just exactly what had been happening to all of us hit me square in the face and I no longer feared the roads to come. I knew without a doubt that God's word was true and was reminded of the promises of Psalm 23, 'Thy rod and Thy staff, they comfort me'. I didn't need some shepherd to make me feel like a real Christian, not ever again. I was free!

"Brother Wendall is a false shepherd and has led God's innocent people into his own brand of religion and called it holy. May the Lord help him on the day of judgment. I've been foolish to stay as long as I have. I'll never go back to that place as long as I live and I pray for all who stay there. I pray for the light of God to shine in that place, and lead His people out of there." If ever there were a time when I felt the Holy Spirit speaking through me, it was now, for surely these were not my own words. Mine would have been spoken in a timid and quiet way, but somehow the Lord seemed to be putting the words into my mouth. I prayed that those words would be received with the love that was intended toward these people who meant so much to me. But even the fear of losing their friendship was not worth the price that would be paid if I remained in that den of iniquity known as the House of Praise!

"Well I think I need the counsel of Sister Parker right about now. Her wisdom has guided me through some tough times and I trust whatever she says!" Sister Dolly marched purposefully and directly toward the avocado green phone hanging on the wall in the kitchen.

"Well Dave, I guess you told the tale." Paul said somberly.

"I guess so." I answered, hoping I'd not done irreparable damage to our relationship. "I suppose I had best get on back home. I know you and your mom have a lot to discuss." I didn't wish to intrude on a private talk between mother and son. He and his mother shared the same closeness I did with my own mom.

"See ya man . . . God bless you." Paul said rather sadly.

"God bless you, too. See ya later." I said walking out of the kitchen door. I could hear his mom on the phone responding to Sister Parker.

"Yes, yes, I knew the Lord would give you a special insight as he always does!" Sister Dolly waved the dishtowel and nodded goodbye to me as I started down the driveway to my car.

As I walked into the comfort of my little house on Linda Lane, the familiar western 'Bonanza' could be heard coming from the living room. I'd not allowed myself this relaxing pleasure in a long time, fearing attacks from Satan if I so much as looked at a television program that didn't "line up" with the word of the gospel-according-to-brother-Wendall.

"C'mon and sit down in here with us, Son. We got a good program on." Daddy said to me as he sat up on the sofa. "Ben Cartwright's just about to go get little Joe out of another jam!" He added excitedly.

I sat down in my old familiar chair, but this time it felt somehow more inviting and more relaxing than ever before.

"Here Son, have a fresh cup of hot coffee." Mama said smiling down at me.

"Thanks, I think I will." I said, allowing myself the little comforts that previously had been denied me. It felt good to once more be in the company of my family, doing something as normal and mundane as having a cup of coffee and watching a television show without being hammered with guilt and fear.

However, in the days that followed, I found myself more exhausted than ever. I was barely able to work my shift at the grocery store before coming home and crashing, sleeping for hours on end, while only waking up for long enough to eat. My mind seemed to be in a sort of soft, hazy fog, which somehow brought a strange comfort to me. I prayed that I would return to my previous "normal" state. But there was some sort of invisible line that existed deep within my soul which drew a separation between what was normal and the place I now found myself in. Similar to AD and BC, time was somehow divided in my mind as before the House of Praise and after the subsequent exit. I prayed the Lord would heal and deliver me so I could once again feel like a normal, whole person rather than the segmented frame of mind I now struggled through daily.

I continued to tell myself that the early days at the fellowship were good and pure. Somehow this line of thinking was more forgiving to my conscience. Even though my family and I had left the place officially, the evil roots and distorted teachings which had been planted would take far longer to remove from our hearts and souls. These were the weeds which would attempt to suffocate the healing, true word of God. The fight had only just begun.

CHAPTER 8

THE JOURNEY HOME

Sitting straight up in my bed, startled by the noise of a rattle trap car with no muffler which had just pulled into our driveway, I wiped the beads of sweat which were rolling down my forehead. This steamy June day was at a full broil as the clock on my dresser ticked half past one in the afternoon. The noisy car backfired and a loud squeak could be heard before the door clanged shut. The metal louvers from the attic fan continued their cantankerous cacophony adding to the misery I felt from the pounding in my head.

"Oh! Why can't we just turn on the air conditioner?!" I mumbled irritably, while straightening my bed. My fuzzy head then remembered that we were saving on the power bill this summer.

"That money machine in the window has got to go! Hard times are ahead and we can certainly do without such luxuries as air conditioners!"

139

Daddy proclaimed from the supper table one night after the power bill had arrived in the mail earlier that same day.

"Gene, get that fire stoked up man! We's gonna have us some chickens for supper!" The voice of my uncle Bubby soared above the racket of the attic fan.

The driver of the contraption once known as a car, slowly made his way into the sparkling clean kitchen with his dirty boots.

"Bub! It's so good to see you! How about a cup of coffee?" The day was never too hot for a cup of coffee with my mother, nor was the "no shoes in the house" rule ever observed by her brother. In all my memory, I could never recall Uncle Bubby having either a working vehicle or clean shoes. Both these observations completely escaped my mother's eyes, as her older brother could do no wrong in her book, and was often quoted as a man with knowledge in many important matters.

"Coffee, I should say not Sister, but I'll go and get a couple uh' cold beers out the trunk of my car and see if I can get Gene to have one with me." He said with glee in his eyes as they darted upon me, in hopes of an objection. It seemed to give him much joy to subtly question my convictions, but I didn't feel up to reacting to his comment today. Besides, I was fond of my Aunt Agnes, his wife and didn't want anything to come between us. A wonderful piano player, she was the one who had originally inspired me to learn the instrument. A deeply religious woman, she had played Christmas carols at our family gatherings during the joyful season, as we sang along. When I was only seven, I used to secretly wish I could play like her.

However, my aunt's polar opposite, Uncle Bubby had come over to help us slay the un-suspecting chickens in our back yard today. Bringing me back to the present, my dad entered the house rubbing his hands together and grinning. "Uh oh, here comes the work." I mumbled to myself.

"Dave, you go out and unlock the shed and get my hatchet out. Time to get busy on 'operation chicken harvest'!" My dad barked out enthusiastically. "And put a smile on your face for crying out loud! These are going to be the best chickens you ever did eat!"

"Yes sir,." I answered trying to manage a smile as I could feel my upper lip curling over my teeth in what surely must have been more of a sneer.

The thought of slaughtering the helpless chickens that I had fed and cared for, was less than appealing to me. I also still missed our dog, Gigi, who was given away to Brother Douglas after a family discussion had brought us to the conclusion that the dog would be 'better off elsewhere.' However, after our exodus from the House of Praise, there didn't seem to be any real point in continuing this 'charade' of a coming apocalypse and the ensuing starvation unless we all grew our own food. So here we were, about to rid ourselves of the birds once and for all.

"Yee haw, you got some pretty birds Gene, I'll say that much for ya!" Uncle Bubby said, lifting the baseball cap to scratch his balding head. "Let me blow my nose first." The same filthy hankie I remembered from a hunting trip long ago came out of his blue work pants.

"It's a wonder that thing doesn't get up and walk" I said a bit too loudly.

"What's that, boy?" Uncle Bubby said, turning to me right after he finished honking like a goose into the soiled bit of cloth and stuffing it back into his pocket.

"I said it's a wonderful day for a walk." I quickly justified to my conscience that this statement was close enough to the truth.

"Huh, well, yeah, I guess so, but you ain't walkin' nowhere but over here to help, boy." Uncle Bubby bellowed loudly enough for all the neighbors who now appeared to be gathering in their back yards to watch the upcoming slaughter.

I took my post awaiting my "gopher-orders." The sheer horror of watching these beautiful birds have their heads whacked off and then their bodies slung over the pin to the ground where they jumped and writhed as though in agony brought me grief, which I tried not to show. I struggled to bring my mind to happier days; days spent with Gigi playing on the beach in the frothy salt waves of the Gulf of Mexico on a Sunday afternoon, after mass.

I turned my head away and saw our neighbor out shaking her rugs harder and a little longer than necessary. This particular neighbor always had rugs to shake when something of interest was going on at our house. Today, her mouth was wide open in blissful curiosity.

"Gene, let's go pop the top on a cold one! I think we both deserve a good brew about now! We did man's work!" Bubby said winking at me. "Dave, c'mon and have one with us. Oh no, I forgot, you probably want milk instead, huh boy? Hehehe." My Uncle cackled.

Choosing to ignore his obvious barb, I instead opted for a cool shower, to wash away not only the day's sweat and grime and blood from the chickens, but also my own memories of the slaughter. Somehow a shower seemed to help put me in a better frame of mind.

The weeks passed quickly enough though and, for the first time in our lives we'd not been to church in a recent Sunday. From the time I was a small toddler, we had been taught that when Sunday rolled around, the family went to church. Missing the religious service on Sunday was not an option. "All the Lord asks from us is one hour a week, and it's the least we can do to give Him our un-divided attention during that hour." My father often said to us as we drove home from St Thomas.

"Pass the bowl of cucumbers son." Daddy asked with his mouth still full from the last bite of tomatoes and cucumbers he'd stuffed in. Our table recently consisted of ever more radishes and cucumbers or tomatoes from our own garden, along with the main course for supper.

"Um, Daddy, I've been doing some praying and something has come to me. You know it's been a while since we've been to any sort of church service." I threw in as I passed the full bowl of cucumber wedges. "I believe the Lord has given me a good idea about that'. I had broken the silence.

"Well, let's hear it Dave!" Daddy said enthusiastically.

"We could have a get together right here at the house and Paul could bring over his guitar. We'd sing a few choruses and do a short study from the Word here in our own living room. I'd practice learning some of the choruses on the piano and play along with them. We'd invite Sister Dolly, and Sister Parker and, of course, Cindy and Karla. Oh, and I could ask Mrs. Tate if I see her at the grocery store which I usually do", I said happily as I sat back to wait on their opinion.

"Well now, I don't know." Mama said doubtfully.

"I think we can manage that, huh Mama?" Daddy added in agreement with me, much to my joyful surprise!

"Yeah, I like the sound of that Dave! I could help in singing the chorus's." Cathy quickly added.

"Well now, I was still wanting to go over to that little church in Pass Christian that Clarice told me about." Mama said rather woefully.

"Oh Mama, please! You listen to her way too much. You have no idea if that place is even Spirit-filled or not. Do you want to go back to the way things used to be with a boring old preacher and a boring old sermon?" Cathy added, unwilling to return to what was now deemed as an all together un-Christian existence.

"Well that don't matter none! Just so long as they preach Jesus!" Mama added in defense of her idea which went over with the family about like a hill full of ants at a Sunday picnic.

"It wouldn't hurt none just to give this a try once, would it now?" Daddy asked, almost pleading with Mama.

The old lessons of the House of Praise wouldn't die easily as the mandates of submission were ominously in the room.

"Well, I guess I could bake a few cookies if y'all are so set on it." Mama grumbled. "But I still say that little church in the Pass is where we ought to be! Clarice done told me that preacher there was just as Spirit filled as they come and I believe her too!" Mama threw in for good measure. If I knew my mother, this would not be the last we would hear of 'that little church in the Pass' as Pass Christian was called by all the locals. Mama had a way of re-visiting subjects of particular interest to her, in which she usually got her way, sooner or later.

The past words of Wendall still rang in my head at times, "the door to Long Beach" and I couldn't help but hold out the hope that this could yet be that door, just in a different way than I had previously thought! This could be the start of something really important in all of our lives!

"Ok, so what night of the week do we want to do this?" I asked Daddy, assuming the matter was already settled, with Mama being the only dissenting voice.

We decided on Saturday night, since the people we invited were used to going to the House of Praise on that night anyway. Paul had arrived early, with a smile on his face and his guitar in tow.

"Hey folks, praise the Lord! I'm ready to sing and play for Jesus and hear some of the Word!" He added joyfully. Cathy was already perched on the floor, sitting Indian style, ready to sing along with the music. I hadn't seen her smile like this in a very long while.

"Oh by the way, my Mom can't come tonight. She and my step father are busy entertaining some of our relatives." Paul added while strumming the a familiar chorus.

"Oh that's too bad." I said, sorry to hear that Paul's mother wouldn't be there. She always brought a ray of sunshine into any room she entered. She had such a sweet and joyful spirit.

"Um, I also know that sister Rhonda and her husband won't be coming. He'd never let her come since you invited sister Tate." Paul added somberly.

"What on earth could be the matter? Sister Tate is one of the sweetest people I've ever met in my life!" I asked incredulous that anyone could possibly have any sort of conflict with this kind woman of God.

Paul had a rather bemused look on his face as though trying to come up with a decent reason.

"Well Dave, you know she *is* black. It's a well accepted fact that some people just don't want to associate with them on any level." My dad said quietly as though the neighbors might be listening. "Even though the Lord has shown us better than that." He added at the last minute.

"I just can't believe that any real Christian would be that closed-minded this day and age! Why that's like something out of the Civil War era, not the 1970's for crying out loud!" I said angrily.

"You mean 'the War between the States.' That's what I've always heard tell it's supposed to be called." My mother added.

"I don't care what it's called, I call it stupid! How dare anyone think of themselves as a Christian and treat someone like dear, sweet, Sister Tate that way! Makes me so mad I could spit!" Cathy added, her temper flaring up.

"The whole point of being a Christian is to love everyone. Sister Tate is one of easiest people to love I ever met! Why I never even think of her as being black.

She's a child of God and I'm proud to know her!" I couldn't help but add my own heartfelt thoughts. If that was the way that man was, then I'd just as soon he kept his prejudiced self and his wife at home, where they belonged . . . locked up tight!

The clock on the wall ticked ever louder as the time passed and no one we had invited showed up.

"Well Dave, you tried. I gotta give you that." Daddy added to try to cheer me up.

"Now can we go on over and visit that little church in the Pass?" Mama had to add, hoping to push that petition through on the heels of this failure.

Just then car lights beamed into our little house. A guest!

"Well, hello Mr. and Mrs. Woods. I hope I'm not too late for the Bible study. I had to drive all the way to Gulfport to drop my granddaughter off at a relative's house so I could come tonight." Mrs. Tate said as she entered the house, Bible in hand and a genuine, loving sweet smile on her face.

"No, not at all Sister Tate! We're just happy to have you join us! You come on in here and have a seat." My dad offered. Soon the entire room was filled with a warmth and love that only the sweet spirit a true child of God can bring. This kind lady exuded everything that a Spirit-filled Christian was supposed to offer to others and she was a most welcome guest!

"Oh Dave, what a lovely piano you have there. I didn't know you played." Sister Tate said as she seated herself next to the piano.

"I'm re-learning it. I used to play as a small boy years ago. Wanna start out with a scripture chorus?" I asked the small gathering.

"Oh that's a good idea Dave. We sang some of those last night at the monthly gospel meeting. You should come sometime. You would hear some very powerful preaching and the Lord moves in wonderful ways there!" Sister Tate offered. "And they sing many of those great new choruses at the Tanner's weekly prayer meetings, too. The Tanner's are just about the most Godly people you will ever meet this side of heaven! They have blessed me time and again. I'm just glad there a so many places we can go to these days to receive a blessing from God.

Mrs. Tate's face had a soft glow about it, almost as though encircled by light. "Dr. Tanner has the best personality and just makes the scriptures come alive when he reads from the Bible. After the meeting is over, Mrs. Tanner has a lovely buffet set up in her dining room for everyone to take part in and just enjoy fellowshipping one with another. Oh, there's young and old alike. The ages seem to make no difference. Everyone there is on an equal footing. She then began to sing a song about Christians being brought together as one in the Lord.

Mrs. Tate sang that chorus with hands open to the heavens. The love she felt for both her Lord and fellow Christians showed in her face, made lovely by the light of God's own presence. This was the real love of God, right here in this woman. God had truly sent her to our home this night.

I'd remembered my friend, Brother Larry from the House of Praise mentioning the Tanner's prayer group. However, brother Wendall, our shepherd, had strictly forbidden us to go there. Now that I was out from his covering, I was free to go wherever I pleased! The thought brought release to my spirit! I felt as though I'd just walked out from an overcrowded room, into the soft spring air!

"How do I get there and what time does it usually start?" I asked quickly.

"Oh my, you are an eager one, Dave. Well good enough. I tell you what, you just follow the railroad tracks till you get to the Pass, then go over them and turn right. The Tanner's home is the old antebellum house on the left about a mile down the road. You can't miss it. It's sure to be lit up and the yard filled with lots of cars. The meeting starts at seven, but everyone gets there a bit early just to fellowship. Oh Dave, this is so exciting! I can't wait to see you there. Oh, and bring some sheet music. They have a piano, and it would be great if you could play for the singing." She asked, taking a sip of her hot coffee and politely setting it down upon her saucer. Mama had prepared a pot of coffee and a plate of homemade chocolate chip cookies for the little bible study. I had sampled a few of them straight out of the oven a few hours earlier, and still remembered savoring the delicious taste.

"Mizz Tate, have you ever been out to that little community church in the Pass? My sister's told me all about it and I'm tryin' to get Gene to take me." Mama half pleaded with Mrs. Tate in hopes of sealing the deal and finally getting her way in the matter.

"Oh, brother here we go." I heard Cathy mumble quietly as she sat beside me and rolled her eyes.

"The preacher there is Brother Beasley, a wonderful man of God, filled with the Holy Spirit! He sings and plays his guitar and you'd swear there was an angel singing instead of a man. He is so kind and has a lovely wife with several children. I do believe there is a girl just about your age, Cathy dear." Mrs. Tate offered.

"There is?" Cathy's entire attitude brightened at this offering. The prospect of meeting other young people seemed to change her opinion of the little church.

Mrs. Tate regaled us with countless stories of charismatic meetings and churches dotted all about the Gulf Coastal area. Just then the clock chimed loudly, 9:00.

"Oh my but the time has just flown by this evening!" Mrs. Tate said as she slowly stood to her feet. "I have got to go pick up my granddaughter and get her home and in the bed!" She brought her coffee cup over to the kitchen sink.

"No, now you just leave that to me Mizz Tate! We'll take care of all that." Mama insisted.

"It's been a lovely evening Mr. and Mrs. Woods. I hope to see you again real soon now. Goodnight to all and God bless!" Mrs. Tate said, waving her hand as she walked out the screen door which smacked loudly behind her.

"I think I'll tag along with you when you go to the Tanners or the gospel meeting, Dave." Paul said as he put his guitar carefully back in its case. "Our family has been relying completely on our old church for all of our spiritual food. I must confess, even though our preacher tries, it does get a bit dry."

"Yeah, that'd be great man. You and me and Cathy can go to the Tanners next Thursday night." I said, with new hope building inside my heart. From that day forward, the little Thursday meeting would always simply be referred to as, 'the Tanners' any time we mentioned it.

The following Thursday night the three of us pulled slowly into the well lit front yard of an old white home with deep mossy green shutters. Candles hung from trees and lined the front steps leading to the brick paved front porch complete with matching deep green rocking chairs and giant purple hydrangeas in earthen pots placed by the front door. The smell of the magnolias and honeysuckle floated in the air, making for a fairy-like forest dream.

"Wow!" I uttered as we got out of the car.

"Yeah and double wow! Did you ever seen anything like this?" Paul said.

"Nope, not me." I looked over at Cathy who was transfixed by the beauty. Cathy loved flowers and couldn't help reaching out to touch a delicate rose growing in front of our parked car.

"It's like something out of a fairy tale," Cathy said smiling and walking slowly toward the front porch.

"It seems the house is just welcoming us in, doesn't' it?" Paul said following behind with his guitar.

"Well hello there! I'm Ouida Tanner. Come right inside! Jim, we have some new guests arriving. Jim's my husband and the teacher at our little gathering." A small framed woman with black hair and striking blue eyes answered the door.

A man with salt and pepper hair and a smile the size of the half moon that hung in the starry summer sky wheeled over to the front door to greet us.

"Well, we're always glad to have some nice young folk join in our group. Come on and make yourselves at home." Dr. Tanner said as he faced his wheelchair toward us. "Doc Jim Tanner here." Dr. Tanner extended his hand in a friendly hand shake.

"I'm Dave Woods and this is my sister, Cathy and our friend Paul." I offered as I shook his hand shyly.

"Well I see you play the guitar, Paul. I strum a little myself. You'll have to join in and help us out with the music." Dr Tanner said brightly.

"Thanks; I think I'll give that a try while we praise the Lord together! Dave here plays the piano and Cathy can sing." Paul offered while shaking the doctor's hand.

"Well fine! We can have us a real sing-a-long then!" Doctor Tanner said as he wheeled into the great room. "Our regular piano player had called and said she couldn't make it, so this is an answer to prayer!"

The fireplace was spilling over with lush, deep green ferns and lights danced off of the creamy colored plaster walls from the sparkling chandelier that hung gently and swayed slightly as someone walked in the room just above. The tinkling of the crystals sounded like a wind chime in the distance on a breezy summer afternoon. The smell of fresh brewed hot coffee and chocolate chip cookies greeted us from the long wooden table that sat in the middle of the dining room which adjoined the great room. A tea colored lace table cloth covered the battered wood which had been through many generations of use. The lace curtains in the oversized French windows and doors all spilled onto the dark, rich heart pine floors. A small upright piano sat in the corner of the room beside the dining room entrance.

"Hello, and welcome! Come and have some coffee and cookies before we settle in for the prayer meeting." Another voice greeted us from a lady who smiled and nearly danced with joy over to the table to assist us in filling cups and saucers with goodies. "Praise the Lord, it's good to have you young people here tonight."

Everyone here seemed to beam with the joy of the Lord! It seemed rather foreign, the thought of being joyous after all I'd been through at the House of Praise, but everyone appeared genuine enough. Perhaps with time, I too could learn to be joyful once more. Putting the past to rest might take time and effort, but I had to try and this was certainly a great place to start!

"Let's all settle in now and sing some choruses to get things started this fine night." Doctor Tanner said as he wheeled himself in front of the fireplace which faced the sofas and chairs that were now quickly filling with friendly faces. "Dave, why don't you and your friend Paul there join along? Paul you can strum that guitar of yours and Dave, you can sit at that old piano and play along."

I nervously approached the piano, not knowing if I yet had the skills to keep up with the music. "Lord help me." I mumbled to myself. "I'm not sure I know the ones that y'all sing or not."

"Well why don't you just play a few that you know then." Doctor Tanner offered.

"Dave, let's do that one about God's kindness," Paul suggested already unbuckling his guitar case.

"Oh that's a grand one! We sing it over at Brother Bill's prayer group and preaching, too!" The lady with the salt and pepper hair said grinning and clapping. I wondered if this friendly woman could possibly be the famed 'prophetess' that Brother Wendall had mocked so many months ago.

"Ok, here goes." I said as my hands stretched out to play the simple chorus.

I heard my sister Cathy's voice ringing out clear as a bell as she wove in and out of the melody adding inflections of harmony here and there. The effect was beautiful as I listened to everyone worshipping the Lord with hands raised, my friend Paul at my side, strumming his guitar skillfully.

We sang several more and then the room fell quiet with anticipation as Doctor Tanner opened the worn, black leather Bible on his lap, as his aging hands lovingly caressed the yellowed pages.

"You know the world has a lot of ideas that are at odds with the teaching of our Savior. For example they are always saying, 'We gotta find ourselves.' But then you look at the Bible and Jesus said, 'we gotta deny ourselves.' Of course I'm paraphrasing tonight, so don't try to follow in your Bibles just yet. The world says, 'You need to take care of number one,' but Jesus said 'You need to become a servant if you want to be great in the kingdom of God.' You see, the world's wisdom will always lead you down the broad path. But Jesus wants us to take the straight and narrow path that leads to life. And it's just because He loves us so much. People, we got a great God and a wonderful loving Savior. How could anyone choose to follow any other path?" Doctor Tanner would then grin from ear to ear with a twinkle in his eye as he continued to describe the wonderful attributes of Christ. It was obvious by the expression on the faces of all present that this man was sincere from the bottom of his heart and walked the path of our Lord in his day to day life. He had earned both the love and respect of all in the room, including myself.

The fact that Dr. Tanner was in a wheelchair somehow disappeared while listening to him speak of the Lord. All that seemed to matter was the love and reverence with which he spoke from the word of God so freely and with such conviction. He had a kindness about him that shone through in his voice and gentle countenance.

"Could I have just found a way to be around other Christians without the chains and bondage I've been burdened by? Could I finally be free from the mental anguish of feeling as though demons were infesting my soul?" I asked myself. A spark of hope flared up deep inside and I felt tears start to well up in my eyes. I quickly willed them back down, not wanting anyone to see my emotion.

In what seemed like only moments, the teaching session had come to a close. I was surprised when I looked at my watch to realize he had been speaking for nearly an hour!

"Does anyone here tonight need special prayer for anything?" Mrs. Tanner asked the group after standing up beside her husband placing one hand gently on his shoulder. I couldn't help but notice the tender glance that passed between husband and wife as he patted her hand a couple of times and looked up giving her a quick wink.

"Um, I do." I raised my hand, almost to my surprise. "I have this headache tonight and sometimes my nerves bother me." I added.

"Well come and sit down right here Dave." Mrs. Tanner motioned toward the simple wooden chair that now sat in the middle of the room. "It's just a dining room chair, but we affectionately call it 'the hot seat.'" "Everyone in the room chuckled. "Some wondrous things have taken place right in this chair. The Lord indeed does answer the prayer of his people!"

I slowly rose and came to sit down nervously in front of the crowd, who now came to put their hands upon my shoulders and head and began to fervently pray in agreement for the Lord to lift the headache from me and release me from its grip. The prayer Doctor Tanner offered was brief and to the point, in grateful praise to the Lord for his love and mercy and asked that he heal me this night of whatever the cause of my headaches were. I could feel the energy of each person praying for me, and the love which flowed out of their heartfelt prayers. Beginning to sense the peace of God in my spirit, I felt the Lord had surely brought me here this night.

Several more people sat in the hot seat that night before the meeting dismissed for refreshments.

"Been playing piano long?" I heard a voice from behind me ask. As I turned around, I saw a young man who had not been at the prayer meeting, but rather had quietly slipped down the stairs afterward. With a guitar slung around his shoulder the teenager began to strum a few chords. "The name's Kenny Tanner by the way." He said, flashing the same slightly mischievous grin that belonged to his father, the doctor.

"I took some lessons when I was a little kid, but haven't really played much since." I admitted. By now I had come to the realization that if I wanted to get any better at the piano, I would need additional lessons.

A new excitement sparked within me. Suddenly, I felt I had something to look forward to! I felt as though I had just allowed myself to experience life once more, just a bit. The sensation was similar to that of an arm or a leg that had gone to sleep and then suddenly the blood had begun to flow once more. The tingling reminded me that there is life yet to be lived!

Kenny smiled and raised his leg onto the dining room chair, plopping his guitar onto his knee, twisting the knobs as he plucked the strings to tune the instrument.

"Hey Kenny boy, play something for your ole Daddy, would ya?" Dr. Tanner asked his son as he quickly wheeled up in front of us.

Just then Kenny's small fingers were skillfully playing an old standby hymn of yesteryear. Kenny sang in one key, while Dr. Tanner sang about an octave below, somewhere not quite on key, but fun and pleasant to hear all the same.

Cathy and Paul snickered and gathered around, joining in the fun. At the end of the song, a good laugh was enjoyed by all just as Kenny started in with another old song by a country music legend, which apparently was a favorite of Dr. Tanner. Once again that mischievous grin spread across his face as his eyes twinkled. "Go ahead on boy." He egged Kenny along. "Jim! What in this world are y'all playin' over there?" Mrs. Tanner gave a disapproving frown to her husband. "Now just stop that! Our guests are still here and you singing that song . . . of the world!" Ouida Tanner scolded with one hand on her hip. Still the effect was not very menacing and was obviously of no consequence to Dr. Tanner whatsoever, other than perhaps to encourage him to sing even louder!

"Play it boy." He grinned at his son who happily complied with the request. This grin was not unlike the one of the cat who swallowed the canary.

"Well I just give up is what!" Mrs. Tanner spun around to scurry the rest of the prayer group out of the house, obviously hoping none had picked up on the "worldly" songs that were being played in the corner by the defiant little crowd which obviously enjoyed the singing of these tunes all the more after her admonition!

After we had played several rounds of enjoyable tunes and laughed, I looked around to realize we were the only ones left in the house.

"Cathy it's getting kind of late. We'd best be getting on home now." I said, thinking I couldn't remember the last time I'd actually laughed this much in a very long time.

"Awww, well, I guess so. But it sure was fun and we'll be back next Thursday!" Cathy said as she naturally reached out to hug Dr. Tanner as though she'd known him for years.

"Um Dave, come here for a quick minute, ok?" Mrs. Tanner summoned me from the small antiquated kitchen which was right off of the dining room. I slipped away without either Paul or Cathy noticing as they were both still talking happily with Dr. Tanner.

"Here Dave, slip these into your pocket." Mrs. Tanner said gently as she handed me a small packet of some headache medicine. "You know the Lord can use medicine and doctors for his glory, too. Now if your headache or anxiety comes back, just take a couple of those and relax for a little bit. That should ease the tension, and if the problem persists, well . . . you just come by and see Jim anytime. He can give you a prescription to help you, ok?" Mrs. Tanner's kindness touched my heart. I'd never expected anyone I'd just met to really care about me on such a personal level.

"Thank you. I certainly appreciate it." I answered, hanging my head down as I turned to walk away.

"Oh and Dave, why not bring your sister and Paul over to the Pass Christian Community church this Saturday night? There's a youth meeting there and a singing group from the north Biloxi church and one from Hattiesburg coming. I hear they're very good. You see this prayer meeting is an outreach of the Long Beach Community church and our sister church is the one in Pass Christian which is pastored by Brother Beasley. Oh he is just a precious man of God and Spirit filled and a dear friend of ours as well. So you see we often get word of different activities going on within our groups." Mrs. Tanner added with a smile.

"Yes M'am, thanks. I think we will just do that, um, go I mean, you know, to the Pass Christian youth thing." I answered smiling.

As we walked out into the soft summer night air, I could hear the ocean in the distance. The Tanner's house was not far from the beach and with the breeze blowing from the south; it carried the relaxing rhythms of the seashore to the front porch. What a night this had been. It gave me reason to hope that there was more to life than being heavily burdened with the constant fear of possesion by demons and submission to your shepherd above all else. Yet, the weeds that had taken root within my soul would not uproot so easily. It would require time . . . . time and much love and kindness from the Lord in the form of Godly folks, like the Tanners. I hoped for meeting more such Christians in my life to help heal the open wounds that still needed tending.

The next morning as I cleaned the restrooms at the grocery store, I happened to glance in the mirror. "Oh my God in heaven, who is that?" I mumbled out loud, startled by the gaunt and ragged features of the young man whose image stared back at me. "Is this, . . . me?" I said putting down the sponge and touching the pulled skin about my mouth that seemed to be in a permanent frown. The eyes of this sad creature were so forlorn, that I found myself aching inside to help him somehow.

I reached out and touched the mirror when suddenly I snapped back into reality. "Am I losing my mind? Is this really how I look?" I said out loud beginning to feel shaky and faint inside. Could it be that the hordes of demons I thought had been cast out of me had once again returned and were overtaking my mind and body once more?

"I rebuke you Satan in the name of Jesus! I cast you out to the pit of hell! Be gone from me and never return!" I mumbled quickly, hoping no one would enter the bathroom while I went through my demon exorcism ritual as quickly as I knew how. I felt nauseated and as though I might vomit from the strain.

What was wrong with me? I thought I was a Spirit-filled happy young man, who was finding the right path to follow the Lord! Panic swept over my mind. "I have to go home. I can't be here right now." I said in my thoughts, already making my way to the office to see my boss, Mr. Easterling.

For the second time in a matter of weeks, I had felt that painful sensation of awaking within my spirit, similar to the awakening of a limb, which had long been asleep. The burning and tingling swept through me. It was almost as if my very soul had gone into atrophy and suddenly called upon to live again. The shock was quite painful at first. Only in the past few weeks had I allowed myself, with the help of Paul and Cathy, to venture beyond the confines of life as I had known it at the House of Praise. I felt myself forcefully pulled from the slumber which had overcome my body and soul ever since the life changing event, that fateful night at the fellowship house. My life seemed torn in two these days. I subconsciously categorized everything in my mind as either "before" that night or "after" that night. Nothing had been the same since then. The slumber I'd been in for months had been much like a hibernation of sorts. Now, I felt myself forcefully coming out into the light of day.

"What is it Woods, I'm a busy man you know." The grumpy cigar chewing man in the seersucker suit answered as the tiny door to his 'office' opened. It was little more than an elevated closet with a glass wall around the top whereby he could view most of what went on within his store. Underneath that bear-like appearance, was more of a teddy bear than a grisly. This man had a good heart and was unfailingly kind and fair to all.

"I, uh, well, that is, I'm not feeling well, sir. I think I need to go home today." I said meekly.

"Is that so?" He answered chewing his cigar while scanning me up and down. "Well then what are you doing hanging around here? Go on, go home! Don't spread your germs!" He answered with a wave of his hand. "Here, go get yourself a cola boy, you look like you need one." His voice became kinder as he reached into his pocket and pulled out some change, quickly putting it into my hand. "Now you see to it, you're back here all the earlier tomorrow morning, now you hear?" The gruff exterior once more came up.

"Yes sir. I'll be here, thanks." I answered and then quickly skirted to the side of the office, slipping the coins into the slots and pulling the cold glass bottle from the inside of the buzzing red machine.

The heat and humidity hit me in a burst of warm air as I exited the store's front doors, heading for the parking lot. The waves seemed dark and angry. Ominous clouds bubbled and percolated in the sky which touched the shores. "Better head home before the storm hits," I thought as I turned the key in the car.

A familiar commercial was on advertising one of my favorite soft drinks. Taking another swig of the one Mr. Easterling had bought for me, I began the short drive home.

"Ok, so maybe that's the message of the day." I had to slightly grin. Perhaps I was yet again, taking life a bit too seriously as I had a tendency to do. My father had told me to just relax sometimes and enjoy the simple things life offered.

"Davey boy, what are you doing home so early?" Mama said, seeing me drive up the driveway as she rocked in the old green rocking chair on the porch.

"Just tired today, that's all. I think I'll take a shower and have a nap before supper." I said going straight inside after taking off my shoes and putting them in the neat row beside the screen door.

After the refreshing shower, my entire body sank into the comfort and privacy of my bed in the little room on Linda Lane. That tiny room that was so familiar to me offered shelter from the now approaching thundershower.

Normally storms rattled my nerves, but not this time. Strangely enough, I felt the tension flowing out of my body as the rain drops slapped the window pane above my bed. "Lord, you are in control of this storm and you are in control of my life. I give it all to you, dear God." I whispered as my mind drifted off in a velvet fog, my eyes fluttering as I gave myself up to a deep sleep.

The following night was the big Saturday evening concert for teens at the Pass Christian Community church. I noticed Cathy had fixed herself up nicely for the event as though she was beginning to enjoy life again as well. She had so often looked sad and melancholy when we were involved with the House of Praise.

"Wow the parking lot of this little place is jammed up!" Paul said as we pulled slowly into the unfamiliar but friendly looking little church.

"The Joy of Jesus Singers" was painted on the side of a small moving trailer, which was parked to the rear of the church.

"Here we go." Cathy said to me as we walked through the doors of the church, which was already abuzz with excited teens milling about everywhere, laughing and talking with one another.

"That's the minister, Brother Beasley." Cathy whispered quietly as the service began, referring to the middle-aged man with curly hair and gentle eyes. She had visited one Sunday morning before with Mama.

"And since I know you kids are ready to get started, with no further ado, I will turn this service over to our friend from our sister church in Biloxi, Brother Bill. Come on up here, Brother Bill." Pastor Beasley encouraged the gathering to offer a friendly round of applause for the portly, smiling man.

"Thank you, and we will all offer Jesus that round of praise, Amen? . . . Amen!" The man had laughter gleaming from every inch of his face. "We just want to have fun tonight in the presence of our Lord and enjoy the music from our youth group which has already lined up and is about ready to fire one up! Let's sing for the Lord!" Brother Bill made a slight bow at the waste to the young people who looked back at him with a fatherly love in their faces.

The little choir began singing a song which exclaimed that Jesus was the answer to all life's many questions.

The simple song sung from the hearts of these young people spread like wildfire through the audience. I dared to glance about and noticed some of them swaying with eyes closed, others even lifted hands in worship, but all wore smiles as the sincere singing melted hearts and lifted up the Lord to all present.

"Hey Dave . . . I think we just found it! This is the real thing, man." Paul leaned over and whispered excitedly to me.

"Yep, I think you're right." I allowed myself to loosen up and enjoy the music and the energy from all the people in the room, all of whom obviously loved the Lord, but did not show the yokes of bondage on their faces that I had become accustomed to.

The youth group sang a few more catchy and upbeat songs before turning the podium over to the main attraction, the group from Hattiesburg called "the Joy of Jesus" singers.

This was a well rehearsed group of young people complete with a young preacher who, between songs, would take the microphone and relate a story about the Lord to us. He did so with great enthusiasm and even laughter, a sound which had become foreign to me. Not one word of discipleship, order, or submission, ever crossed anyone's lips this night.

The songs were sung with expertise and sincerity. What joy filled my heart at the sound of the words! I wanted THIS . . . THIS was what I'd been searching for all along and now, thank the Lord I'd found it!

After many songs had been sung, each one leading to a more reverent feeling that flowed through the tiny church, the pews packed shoulder to shoulder with young people, the preacher once more took the microphone. This time his voice was quiet as a soft breeze on the evening tide and just as soothing:

"If anyone has a need, I want you to make your way to the front of the church now. The Lord is surely in this place!" The short framed man with the large mustache took out his handkerchief and dabbed at the perspiration that gathered on his brow. "If you need to ask Jesus into your life for the first time, or if you've been a Christian for years and would like a closer walk, please, right now, just come and pray. If you're worried or there is a lot of anxiety in your life, come forward and the Lord will minister to your needs." He seemed to be looking directly at me with those piercing eyes. "Just grab the hand of the person next to you and ask them to come with you. They'll come!"

Every muscle in my body was compelled to walk up to the front and pray. "Paul, can you . . ." I leaned over and quietly asked my friend.

"I'm with you man." Paul finished the sentence and had risen even before me to make the short walk down to the front which was already being flooded with young people, some standing with heads bowed, others kneeling and others still with uplifted hands and tears streaming down their sunlit faces.

Faith had risen in my heart that God could begin to help me through these attacks of anxiety that had plagued me for so long now. As I knelt to the floor near the altar, tears had already begun to stream down my face. God's Spirit was touching my soul even as others gathered around me to pray. My eyes caught a glimpse of Sister Tate gently putting her hand on my shoulder nodding in agreement to seek the Lord with me. In the background, I could hear the words being sweetly and softly sung. The quiet and peaceful presence of God reiterated to words to the song, which also spoke of finding a special place in your heart for the Lord.

As I knelt there in prayer, a sweet release and surrender flooded my soul in such a real way, that I wanted to linger there forever. Slowly, one by one, each made their way back to the pew from which they had come. I arose and wiped the tears from eyes to see the tender and kind smile of Dr. Tanner, sitting in his worn wheelchair, who had been behind me, silently praying the entire time. Warmth filled me from within to know I'd found such friends, right in my own back yard, and they were genuinely following Christ, each in their own way. Now they were becoming my friends. Glancing to the back of the little church, I spotted my parents, too. My mom had finally gotten to come again to the 'church in the Pass.' I wondered now why we had given her such a hard time about this simple little request of hers.

After the service, the floodgates of new friends embraced us as the teenagers all introduced themselves and invited us to join them for a bite to eat at a local restaurant. Brother Bill, who the kids affectionately called "Papa" joined in the laughter and was truly loved and respected by one and all. I even saw Cathy doing some of her impersonations which she gladly performed since she was a little girl. What a knack she had for making others laugh. Her laughter rang out like a bell among the other kids. I'd not often heard that laugh for nearly a year now.

Brother Beasley, Sister Tate, Brother Bill and the Tanners were among the most sincere and kind heart hearted people of God I'd ever met in my life. I'd come to know them within the course of these few short weeks, and they were gently showing me that I could fulfill the desire of my heart and serve the Lord *with gladness*!

This confidence and joy filled my soul. No longer was I the naïve boy who visited the House of Praise a year ago. Cindy had once said that the highest form of worship was through singing high praises. Could it actually be that at least one of the highest forms of worship to God was to live an ordinary life in service to Him? Although the experiences at the fellowship house had at times been dark and terrifying, God was indeed fulfilling his promise by working all things for the good to those that love the Lord.

In my senior year of high school, a painfully shy boy had made the decision to follow Christ . . . . but now . . . I was beginning to see that He was the one who was guiding me, keeping my feet on the path of the straight and narrow road which leads to eternal and everlasting life with Him!

And then as if a gentle breeze blew through my mind, a song came to me. It was just a simple melody, but one that was surely running through my head just as the waters run through a gentle stream. As I concentrated on the words, I drifted into a wonderful daydream. Most folks would find that an ordinary experience and I guess it is. But I was beginning to learn that it's the ordinary joys of everyday life that God indeed intended for His children.

EPILOGUE

Many years have gone by since the events that took place in this story. Although the road to recovery was slow, God's hand has always been evidenced in my life and even in the lowest of times, there was always an assurance deep inside, that all I needed to do was reach out to Him in prayer.

I decided to tell my story because as a result of the *trials* God allowed me to go through; I learned a profound truth at a very young age. Are you ready for this? It's perfectly ok to be ordinary. Paraphrasing the words of Christ, He wants us to have life more abundantly.

Cults have preyed on the young and vulnerable for years and, unfortunately, their leaders are getting wiser as time go by. In the church world today, they usually mix a whole lot of truth with just a little error.

The first thing these cult leaders try to do is get their followers to believe that they have an exclusive truth which no other Christian group has ever been enlightened to. Some even discourage visitation to other churches. Once they've isolated their group, they can gradually bring in more deception incrementally. Most of the modern leaders use the Bible as their foundation, but they rarely teach doctrine from lengthy passages. They prefer to isolate a verse or two and build their entire belief system on a passage taken out of its intended context.

They usually prey on the seemingly gullible and naïve, hence there are often a disproportionate number of young people as opposed to intact families. I like to see a healthy variety of age groups when I enter a church or Bible study. The size of the crowd makes absolutely no difference, though.

To this very day, I get an uncomfortable feeling when a preacher puts forth the attitude that his words are not to be questioned because he's teaching "the Word of God". God's Word is indeed perfect, but arrogance is not the way of Christ. The Holy Spirit is gentle and He guides His people with patience. Any and all men have imperfections. A true man of God will admit his own fallibility to the congregation.

Listen to your instincts, because God gave them to each of us for a reason. Balance everything with your own daily devotions, prayer and reading of the Bible for yourself.

When I was first delivered from the cult I had become involved with, the thing that stood out most in the churches I visited afterwards was the focus of their teaching. Their emphasis was on the Gospel of Christ, and He alone was lifted up above all else. Unhealthy churches will always exalt their own particular teaching or "revelation" more than they lift up the Lord Jesus Christ.

If you've found yourself in chains of bondage to one of these cult groups, there is hope. Think the un-thinkable. Be like the man who found himself in a snake handling church way back in the hills. Make your own back door! Listen to that still small voice of God. Leave as soon as possible, though.

Once you've made that exit, re-connect with family and friends if you've lost that relationship. Family was given to us by the Lord and we're all blessed to have them. Stay in fellowship at a church which really does center on the gospel of Christ, his crucifixion and His resurrection in the way that He presented it. Read the Sermon on the Mount. Its truths are profound and actually quite ordinary. Isn't it great to feel normal again? It surely was for me.

In 1979, I wrote the words to this song which was later recorded by' Rejoice', the band mentioned in the prologue.

> It's a new day, and I've just gotta say,
> That knowin' Jesus makes me feel so glad
> And each new day, I take His lovin' hand
> He's got control, Joy fills my soul
> It's so good to be a part in God's plan

Whatever path God leads you on, take His hand and walk with Him each day, because that road will someday lead you home.

ABOUT THE AUTHORS

David Gervais

Born in the heart of Dixie to a blue-collar family during the fun 1950's, David grew up in a sleepy southern town on the tropical Gulf of Mexico. He still enjoys the small town life in a little village not unlike one of his favorite 1960's television shows.

Among his many interests, David enjoys writing, reading, is an accomplished pianist and has mastered numerous instruments. He enjoys playing the piano for his local church and at other Christian functions as well as teaching adult Sunday school and various activities with the local youths.

David is currently an active host family for international exchange students as well as an adoptive foster parent.

David's current occupation is a full time warehouse manager for a major distribution corporation. He eagerly looks forward to retirement whereupon he can dedicate more time to his love of music and writing.